What people are saying about Tom Brown and *Breaking Toxic Soul Ties*...

"I have known Pastor Tom Brown for many years. He is well-grounded in the Word of God and highly respected as a pastor, teacher, and author. I am pleased to endorse *Breaking Toxic Soul Ties,* with the knowledge that it will be a life-changer for those who read it and apply its principles."

—*Dr. Larry Ollison*
President, International Convention of Faith Ministries (ICFM)

"There are many misconceptions people can have when reading the title of this book: *Breaking Toxic Soul Ties: Healing from Unhealthy and Controlling Relationships*. These can be formulated based on doctrinal predispositions, vague familiarity with the concept of "soul ties" from reading articles or books, or perhaps simply allowing yourself to dismiss the entire concept as unnecessary because you personally don't feel it is an area of need. Let me challenge you to put those misconceptions aside and allow yourself the opportunity to receive some of the most balanced, scriptural, and helpful information I've ever read on this topic. I urge you to read it so you can help others; however, I am firmly convinced that as you read, you will be helped in some facet of your own personal life and spiritual development. Tom Brown's extensive ministerial and pastoral experience, as well his personal life experiences, have enabled him to do a masterful job of identifying the symptoms of past hurts or wounds that have given birth to potentially destructive relationships. He then gives wise instruction, correction, encouragement, and biblical keys for healing the wounded hearts, minds, and souls of those who have been scarred by past events and entangled in the webs of unhealthy relationships."

—*Reverend Marty Blackwelder*
BlackwelderMinistries.org

"Have you ever heard someone mention 'soul ties' and wondered just what they meant? Or perhaps you feel that you are 'in bondage' with someone who has control over you. Then this book is for you! It is a must-read primer for anyone dealing with negative soul ties. Tom Brown explains the difference between good and bad soul ties, and the various types of manipulation people use—and abuse—on others. Read this book and learn how to free yourself from the bondage of Satan. Live a free and joyful life, and remember, 'No one can defeat you but you!'"

—*Faye G. Hanshew*
President/CEO, Inspired Creations Publishing Company LLC

Have you ever been in a bad or toxic relationship? Have negative people wounded you? Do guilt, condemnation, and a feeling of rejection hold you back? If so, *Breaking Toxic Soul Ties* will set you free from the ungodly soul ties that have been keeping you from God's best. Pastor Tom Brown masterfully explains how to receive inner healing and how to truly forgive those who have hurt you. After you read this book, you will feel like a great weight has fallen off your back and you will be ready to dance.

—*Daniel King*
www.kingministries.com

Tom Brown's book, *Breaking Toxic Soul Ties,* is written with such a refreshing attitude and with a sincerely honest spirit of encouragement that offers help to all. It contains a powerful, rational, and wise spiritual logic that will result in many people finding real restoration of their self-identity and a new confidence in life that is based in the Lord Jesus Christ.

—*Chas Stevenson*
Pastor of Houston Faith Church, Houston, TX

Have you ever read a book that makes you look at your life up close and personal, examining your heart to see who you really are and what you have become? I did this as I read Tom Brown's revealing explanation of soul ties (both good and bad)—my relations with the people in my life or memories of past relationships. This powerful examination of who's who and what's what in your life can have an amazingly positive effect on you for the rest of your life. This is a must-read. I suggest that you have a journal handy to help you really explore these pages, and that you then recommend it to someone else.

—*Dr. Thelma Wells*
Founder, A Woman of God Ministries and Generation Love
Divine Explosion International Conferences
Professor, Speaker, Author, Mentor, aka Mama T

In *Breaking Toxic Soul Ties,* Tom Brown identifies the real-life, unseen things that consistently cause you to do what you never intended to do. You know that a single step in the wrong direction will take you down the wrong path, and yet, too often, you end up *going where you don't want to go* and *doing what you don't want to do*! If you are fed up with hurting yourself, your spouse, or, worse yet, your children, who are always watching your habits and practices, this book is required reading. The evil Jezebel spirit is real. You may have heard about soul ties but never associated them with this manipulative spirit. Thanks to Tom Brown, not only will your eyes be opened, but more important, you also will acquire a strategy to limit the influence that this controlling spirit has in your life. Read, share, and educate, and then read the book two more times and see your life is changed for the better as you become forever free from this destructive spirit.

— *Dr. Phillip G. Goudeaux*
Pastor, Calvary Christian Center, Sacramento, CA

Pastor Tom Brown has touched on a very misunderstood subject. Soul ties, both good and bad, are real. If you've ever struggled with unhealthy feelings, inadequacies, or past hurts, this book is exactly what you have been looking for. God wants the best for your life but your past can greatly limit that from happening. Pastor Tom Brown explains how you can break that cycle and live free from the negative effects of unhealthy soul ties, so that you will finally enjoy God's best in your life.

—*Dr. Jim Willoughby*
Senior Pastor, Faith Life Center, Eastvale, CA
Faithlife.center

BREAKING TOXIC SOUL TIES

TOM BROWN

WHITAKER HOUSE

The names and details of some people have been changed to protect their privacy.

Breaking Toxic Soul Ties:
Healing from Unhealthy and Controlling Relationships

Tom Brown
P.O. Box 27275
El Paso, TX 79926
www.tbm.org

ISBN: 978-1-62911-954-0
eBook ISBN: 978-1-62911-955-7
Printed in the United States of America

Whitaker House
1030 Hunt Valley Circle
New Kensington, PA 15068
www.whitakerhouse.com

Library of Congress Cataloging-in-Publication Data
LC record available at https://lccn.loc.gov/2017050550

1 2 3 4 5 6 7 8 9 10 11 𝐖 25 24 23 22 21 20 19 18

CONTENTS

PART III: THE BROKEN SOUL

PART IV: HEALING FOR YOUR SOUL

PART V: HOW TO HANDLE REJECTION

PART VI: DEVELOP SELF-ESTEEM IN CHRIST

INTRODUCTION: WHY DO YOU STAY?

Are you hanging on to a relationship that should have ended a long time ago? Maybe a voice inside is telling you that you should break it off, yet something in your past is pulling you toward this bad relationship.

You were created as a social creature. You need relationships in your life. They are good for you. Interacting with other people is part of God's plan for helping you to grow. Relationships provide the spice to life. Yet the devil will try to bring the wrong people your way in order to bring chaos, distraction, and even destruction into your life. These people are not just casual friends; some of them are people you develop close connections with.

These connections are called *soul ties*.

Not all soul ties are bad. When you were born, you naturally developed soul ties with your parents. If your relationship with them was predominately healthy, then, from these foundational soul ties, you naturally created other good soul ties in your life. For most people, the next soul ties you develop are with siblings, if you have them, or grandparents, aunts, uncles, and cousins. Once you developed good relationships with family, you were likely to develop good relationship with friends—the peers you grew up with in your neighborhood, in school, and later at work. So long as these soul ties are beneficial and healthy, you then create the most important soul tie of your life—with your spouse in marriage.

If, along the road of life, you fail to create and experience these needed bonds with parents, siblings, and friends, you may experience a brokenness in your soul. This brokenness may lead you to find someone who is also broken and create a soul tie with that person. Relationships like this often end in failure. Instead of experiencing a mutually beneficial bond that improves both of your lives, dysfunction develops, and you tear each other down. If one person dominates the relationship, that person will get all the benefits of the relationship, while the weaker person suffers.

Even if you have good bonds with parents, siblings, and friends, the devil may still trick you into a bad relationship. It happens. While your relationship with your parents may be healthy, the devil may use another relative or perhaps even a stranger to abuse you. This abuse, whether sexual or emotional, can damage your soul, and make you increasingly vulnerable to future negative soul ties.

Terri was a preacher's kid. She had great parents and got along well with her sister, yet, tragically, she was raped by a stranger at a water park. Even though it wasn't her fault, shame kept her from telling anyone about the attack, including her parents. She became broken.

In time, the devil brought a young man into her life. He was a Christian, so Terri's parents were not concerned. This man, however, preyed upon her brokenness by being physically abusive. And even though Terri knew it was wrong, she began to have sex with him.

At first, the relationship seemed exhilarating. In time, to make sure Terri didn't get away, the man asked her to marry him. Romantic feelings are the strongest type of love you can feel. Though you *love* your parents, when you are *"in love"* with someone, feelings take over, and things like good judgment and reason are pushed to the side. You are willing to "leave your father and mother" to become united to the person you love. This is how Terri felt. Any instances of physical abuse were justified because the excitement of romance excused the pain—at least for a while. Although his bouts of rage and jealousy caused the physical abuse to continue, she married him anyway.

After the wedding, Terri became a nervous wreck around her husband. She felt completely stifled. He blew up over anything that made him jealous or angry. Nothing Terri did could stop his rage. She was frightened of him. She felt no sense of self-worth. She began to believe that his abuse was her fault, that there was something wrong with her. She was so embarrassed that she could not tell her parents about her living nightmare. She plastered a smile on her face when she went to church, but deep inside, she was crying. She needed freedom.

Eventually, Terri mustered the courage to talk to friends about her marriage. They encouraged her to leave, but she felt a strong attachment to her husband. They had experienced so much together that it was too hard to contemplate life without him.

What was it that kept her bound to such an unhealthy marriage? It wasn't just the fact that, as a Christian, she believed marriage was for life. She knew that although God was against divorce, He was also against the violence of an abusive husband. Something else held her captive to this abusive relationship.

Eventually, she heard the message about ungodly soul ties. She recognized the truth immediately. Her soul was attached to this man, and not just through their marriage covenant, but through something darker. She thought, *Something within me is sick, something that makes me feel shame and worthlessness.* She knew a healthy wife would not put up with a man physically abusing her, but she was not "healthy." Her soul was sick. Then it dawned on her: *the rape at the water park damaged me more than I realized.* It had broken her spirit. A sick soul breaks the human will, and Terri did not have the will to leave. She knew she should, but she couldn't.

Terri finally received healing for her soul, healing that gave her the strength to stand up. Even though she had hoped that her husband would eventually change, Terri was determined not to be his punching bag anymore. She divorced him. (Neither Terri nor I advocate divorce, except in rare occasions, such as adultery, physical abuse, abandonment, and other damaging forms of dysfunction. You should seek advice through trusted and safe sources like your pastor before you decide to take this course of action.)

Terri has remarried a godly man. She now has a ministry for women in which she teaches others how to break their negative soul ties.

The key to Terri's freedom was inner healing. It is not enough that you know you have a negative soul tie; you also need to receive healing to have the willpower to break free. That is what this book is about. It is not just about romantic soul ties, but about any sort of negative soul ties that cause bondage.

This book is divided into six sections:

Part I will help you to differentiate between biblical and abusive forms of authority.

Part II explains more fully what good and bad soul ties are.

Part III will show you how harmful soul ties develop.

Part IV explains the process of inner healing.

Part V tells my story of rejection and the lessons I learned about how to deal with it.

Part VI explores your self-image in Christ. Until you learn to develop a proper self-image as a believer, you will always be susceptible to bad soul ties.

Are you ready to break negative soul ties and experience inner healing? Then have Kleenex handy (you might need it) as we seek to understand your soul ties, and help lead you on the path toward inner healing and freedom.

PART I
BREAKING FREE

ONE

TOLERATING THE JEZEBEL SPIRIT

Is someone in your life influencing you in a negative way? Perhaps you've tried to break free from their negative influence, but you can't. It so, there may be a *Jezebel spirit* controlling your life. A negative soul tie with a Jezebel spirit can destroy a person, a church, and even an entire community.

NO ONE IS IMMUNE TO THE INFLUENCE OF OTHERS

You are a byproduct of the people who influence you. Everyone in one way or another is influenced by others. The people in your life will have an influence on you, either for good or for bad. Consider Solomon's wise words: *"Do not make friends with a hot-tempered man, do not associate with one easily angered, or you may learn his ways and get yourself ensnared"* (Proverbs 22:24–25). People rub off on you. You learn the ways of other people by closely associating yourself with them. If you associate with godly people, their godly ways will rub off on you; likewise, if you associate with ungodly people, their ungodly ways will rub off on you.

"He who walks with the wise grows wise, but a companion of fools suffers harm" (Proverbs 13:20). When God wants to bless you, He sends you a wise person, but when the devil wants to harm you, he sends you a fool. Don't become a companion of a fool.

One important foolish companion that the Bible warns us against is the Jezebel spirit. Jesus mentioned the Jezebel spirit to the church in Thyatira: *"You tolerate that woman Jezebel, who calls herself a prophetess. By her teaching she misleads my servants into sexual immorality and the eating of food sacrificed to idols"* (Revelation 2:20).

I believe that this woman, "Jezebel," was a code word for a certain woman in the church whom the citizens of Thyatira knew. As Jesus dictated His letter to John in Revelation, He did not call her by name, because she was likely an important citizen of the Roman Empire. If He had used her actual name, the authorities may have intervened and destroyed the letter. So, instead, Jesus used the name of a former wicked queen of Israel to describe the type of woman that was in the church.

Yes, even people in the church can have a Jezebel spirit controlling them. Jezebel spirits are not just found in the world, they can also be seen in church. And, the Jezebel spirit is not related only to women—*people of both genders can be controlled by the Jezebel spirit.*

THE JEZEBEL INFLUENCE

Jezebel was a famous queen in the Old Testament who influenced her husband, King Ahab, to stop worshipping God and to begin worshipping many false idols. (See 1 Kings 16:31.) She persecuted and killed God's prophets, and fabricated evidence causing an innocent landowner to be put to death. (See 1 Kings 2:5–25.) Ever since, she has always been associated with false prophets.

Like her, the Jezebel woman at Thyatira was powerful and influential. She called herself a prophetess, and she made herself to be important. Evidently, her self-advertisement worked, because even God's servants were deceived by listening to her teaching. She did not simply lead people into immorality by example, she also taught it.

What did she teach? We get an idea of what she taught in the book of Revelation: *"Now I say to the rest of you in Thyatira, to you who do not hold to her teaching and have not learned Satan's so-called deep secrets"* (Revelation 2:24). The term *"Satan's so-called deep secrets"* is a reference to the Gnostics. They were first-century heretics who denied the incarnation of God in Jesus. One of the main messages of the Gnostics was this: "Since the flesh is sinful, Jesus could not have become flesh. And if flesh is sinful, then it does not really matter what you do with your body." From this false concept came justification for other ideas, such as the fertility temple, where business was conducted, sexual acts were performed, and food sacrificed to idols was consumed. The businesspeople of the town were expected to join in these sexual acts and festivals.

This problem raised an important question within the church. Should Christians conduct business in this fertility temple? Obviously, the answer was no. But Gnostics, believing that the body was evil anyway, convinced God's servants to go along with the festival in the fertility temple, saying that it didn't really matter what you did with your body. The spirit of Jezebel always rationalizes sinful behavior.

YOU DON'T HAVE TO REMAIN THE VICTIM

Jesus pointed out the main problem with the church of Thyatira: *"You tolerate that woman Jezebel."* He did not only criticize the woman, but also the church. It was as much their fault that she was misleading God's servants into immorality as it was the woman's fault. The church should have excommunicated her instead of giving her a platform for her teachings. Thus, Jesus' message was not aimed at Jezebel but at those being influenced by her. It may seem harsh to point the finger at the victims instead of Jezebel herself, but, you see, Jesus believes that at some point, every victim has the power to put a stop to their own victimization.

This book is not written to try to change Jezebel, but rather to keep her from changing you. Jesus saw little hope that the Jezebel spirit would change its ways. He said, *"I have given her time to repent of her immorality, but she is unwilling. So I will cast her on a bed of suffering, and I will make those who commit adultery with her suffer intensely, unless they repent of her ways"* (Revelation 2:21–22).

Jesus is patient, but His patience is not everlasting; we know this because He says He will eventually judge the world. He gives up on any voluntary change from Jezebel, and, instead, puts her on the bed of affliction with the expectation that perhaps she would eventually change because of her pain. However, Jesus offers a way out to those being influenced by Jezebel. He warns the victims that if they don't repent from Jezebel's ways, they will suffer with her. But if they do, there is hope.

JESUS OFFERS A WAY OUT TO THOSE BEING INFLUENCED BY JEZEBEL. HE WARNS THE VICTIMS THAT IF THEY DON'T REPENT FROM JEZEBEL'S WAYS, THEY WILL SUFFER WITH HER. BUT IF THEY DO, THERE IS HOPE.

This message is to you—you are not a victim who can't repent. There are certain *ways* you have picked up from Jezebel. You have tolerated those ways in your life. You shouldn't do so anymore!

The sin of the victims was tolerance. *Tolerance* is a word that usually has a positive connotation. While tolerance can be used in a positive way, there is also an ungodly usage of tolerance. When you tolerate something evil that has a detrimental effect on yourself or others, then the tolerance itself becomes evil.

To tolerate is not necessarily to propagate something. It is simply to allow it to continue without doing anything to stop it. As harsh as it may seem to put this responsibility on the victims of Jezebel, Jesus recognized that they were indeed tolerating negative soul ties caused by the spirit of Jezebel.

Leah Remini was on the hit TV show *The King of Queens*. You would have never guessed that she was a member of a cult—the Church of Scientology. This false religion is the epitome of the Jezebel spirit. They exhibit complete control over their members, as they did to Remini herself.

One day, as she was attending Tom Cruise's wedding, she asked a Scientology official why a certain person wasn't at the wedding. The official rebuked her, and told her that she was not high enough in the church to ask such a question. This began Leah's search for the truth. After investigating her "church," she discovered that it was a false religious cult. No longer a victim, she broke free from the grasp of Scientology. Though she was shunned by many of her friends and relatives for doing so, she also knew that the responsibility for her spiritual journey was her own. She came to believe in Jesus Christ, and now worships the Son of God instead of the leaders of Scientology, and she uses her influence to try to help others get free from that false religion.

Like her, you must take responsibility to break free from the Jezebel spirit. You can't bemoan how unfair it was for you to be lied to in the past. You can't make excuses for allowing the Jezebel spirit to control you. You must break free.

REJECTING AUTHORITY AND ITS INEVITABLE RESULT

Although many people associate Jezebel with sexual promiscuity, there is no example in the Old Testament of Queen Jezebel behaving in such a way. Instead, she is described as a wicked queen who led people into the worship of idols. She had no regard for the rights of individuals. She also usurped authority from her husband.

The greatest manifestation of the Jezebel spirit is the rejection of authority, or the abuse of authority. The greatest authority over us is God. Second in authority is God's Word, the Bible. Whenever someone begins to take issue with the authority of the Bible, they are manifesting the spirit of Jezebel.

God also puts leaders in the church to guide people as another level of authority. *"Obey your leaders and submit to them, for they are keeping watch over your souls, as those who will have to give an account*" (Hebrews 13:17 ESV). Spiritual leaders have to make decisions based on the wisdom God provides for them, including putting other people in charge of various ministries. They must also have the power to discipline others in order to protect the church; otherwise, they are only figureheads. Often, when a person with a Jezebel spirit gets disciplined, he or she begins to rebel. No one likes to receive discipline, but it is sometimes necessary to run the church.

The hardest job I have as a minister is when circumstances lead to the excommunication of a church member. Excommunication should be the last resort that any church takes. It should only take place when the pastor concludes that all attempts at reconciliation and truth-telling have been exhausted and the danger the offender poses to the church far outweighs any hope for restoration. I once had to excommunicate a member when I found out that he had committed adultery with two women in the church I was leading—one of them being just seventeen years old. After confronting him, I discovered that this behavior was a pattern in his life. He had not just committed adultery with these two women, but he had done this numerous times before he ever came to my church.

Pastors cannot put their church at risk. Pastors cannot be overly sympathetic with people in the church who have the propensity to hurt more people. A pastor must not tolerate the Jezebel spirit in the church.

EFFECTS OF THE JEZEBEL SPIRIT

Why is the Jezebel spirit so dangerous? What are some examples of the work of the Jezebel spirit? It brainwashes members of religious groups so they are afraid to act on their own conscience—the Church of Scientology is an example. It binds a wife to an abusive marriage. It endangers a child by keeping him or her in the home of an abuser. It risks taxpayers' money by sheltering political leaders from accountability. It encourages demagoguery in a nation so that minorities and the politically disenfranchised are destroyed or hurt. Hitler exercised the Jezebel spirit when he demonized and tried to exterminate Jews, gypsies, the physically and mentally handicapped, and anyone who stood in his path. It terrifies workers and prevents them from standing up to bosses who break the law. It turns a blind eye toward police brutality against the marginalized or, conversely, overreacts toward police by undermining the authority of those who are simply doing their duties.

YOU NEED TO RECOGNIZE THAT YOU HAVE THE POWER TO END JEZEBEL'S INFLUENCE OVER YOUR LIFE. YOU MUST TAKE A STAND, AND REFUSE TO TOLERATE THE JEZEBEL SPIRIT, EITHER IN YOUR LIFE OR IN THE LIVES OF OTHERS.

HOW TO RESPOND

The victims are partly to blame for the problem with the Jezebel spirit. They allow it to thrive. I know this is not a "feel-good," sweet-and-cuddly message; however, it is exactly the message some of you need to hear.

A pastor can't simply tolerate sinfulness in the church without addressing it. A wife can't simply tolerate an abusive or cheating husband without taking action. Citizens can't simply tolerate demagoguery in their nation without attempting to stop it. Brainwashed members can't simply tolerate a cult; they must get out.

I've written this book because the Jezebel spirit is alive and working in the world and in the church today. In the end, it is your responsibility to stop others from manipulating you, enticing you to sin, or causing you to rebel against true leaders. You need to recognize that you have the power to end Jezebel's influence over your life. You must take a stand, and refuse to tolerate the Jezebel spirit, either in your life or in the lives of others.

TWO

DON'T LET OTHERS CONTROL YOU

The producers of the MSNBC documentary on exorcism wept after I ministered to a young woman, whom I will call Ruth, who was oppressed by demons. They said, "We have never seen anyone receive help like the help you gave to this woman."

Psychologists might have declared Ruth to be mentally ill, but her real problem stemmed from a hidden demonic molestation. Unbeknownst to her mother, Ruth's father had sexually molested her. As I ministered to Ruth, I said, "There is something in your past that you have kept hidden. What is it?"

She turned and looked at her mother, who was off camera, and said, "My father molested me, and my mother did nothing to stop him!"

The mother was shocked. "I didn't know he was doing that to you."

"How could you not know?" asked Ruth. "There were signs all around that he was doing this to me. Can't you see how sick I am? I am sick because of what he did to me!"

Needless to say, we felt the scene was too private to air on TV, so it was cut from the documentary on exorcism. But this story illustrates that the wrong people can wreak havoc in your life. Later in the book, I will continue Ruth's story, and explain how she received inner healing.

POSITIONS OF AUTHORITY

> *Obey your leaders and submit to their authority. They keep watch over you as men who must give an account. Obey them so that their work will be a joy, not a burden, for that would be of no advantage to you.* (Hebrews 13:17)

Willingly putting yourself under the authority of capable and wise leaders is a voluntary act of submission that is biblical. But you should never allow yourself to be controlled or manipulated by others. Soul ties with controlling and manipulative people have a devastating effect.

The apostle Paul wrote, *"You were running a good race. Who cut in on you and kept you from obeying the truth?"* (Galatians 5:7). There might be no greater bondage than that of being under the dominating control of another person. People should respect authority—wife for husband, employee for boss, child for parents—yet even those in places of authority can abuse their God-given responsibilities. Ruth's father abused his position as her father, just as many other people abuse their positions today.

The only person who has the right to completely control you is God! No one else has that right. A person loses their right to control you when they *"cut in on you"* and keep you from *"obeying the truth."* Truth is a greater authority than any human authority.

THE ONLY PERSON WHO HAS THE RIGHT TO COMPLETELY CONTROL YOU IS GOD! NO ONE ELSE HAS THAT RIGHT.

My earthly father was not a believer, and he did not want me to be a committed Christian, let alone a minister. He tried to dissuade me from my walk with God. I always showed respect to him, but I would not allow him to dictate my walk with God. God is always first!

DEMONIC CONTROL

Control is beneficial when it is exercised by those in authority to benefit others. It becomes demonic when a person dominates another's behavior to benefit their own personal desires and security, without any consideration for the welfare of the person they are controlling. Demonic control is selfish!

A good person who sees you running the good race of faith will cheer you on. They will even be inspired to run beside you. They will not try to trip you or jump in front of you to slow you down. No! They are for you, not against you. But controllers want to exercise demonic control. Paul continued to write, *"That kind of persuasion does not come from the one who calls you"* (Galatians 5:8).

Demonic control is persuasive. There is nothing inherently wrong with persuasion. As a minister, I try to persuade people to accept Jesus Christ as Lord and Savior. I do my best to exercise this kind of persuasion. One atheist told me, "You are very persuasive!" She said it in a way that was meant to criticize me. Yet, God will anoint ministers to be persuasive in order to bring people to the gospel!

However, controllers have demonic persuasion that drives people away from *"the one who calls you."* Professors in universities, even Christian universities, can have a demonic ability to persuade people to reject Christianity and favor atheism or secularism. This is demonic influence and it happens all too often.

STAND FIRM IN YOUR FREEDOM

> *It is for freedom that Christ has set us free. Stand firm, then, and do not let yourselves be burdened again by a yoke of slavery.* (Galatians 5:1)

Legal slavery in the US has been abolished for many decades, but illegal slavery is still rampant. Any time people rob you of your freedom in Christ, you are being subjected to slavery. The controller becomes a master; you become the slave. The master tells you how to live, who you can see, and what you can do. The master has undue influence over your life.

Paul said, *"Do not let yourself be burdened again by a yoke of slavery."* It is ultimately up to you to end the yoke of slavery. I hate to say this, but if people manipulate you for their selfish ends, unless you are a child, it is partly your fault! Not that you are to be blamed for their demonic control, but rather for not fighting back. Controllers are bullies. They will continue to bully you until you fight back.

You have to resist their control over you; no one can resist it for you. Others can tell you the truth about how a person is keeping you from your God-given purpose and calling in life, but only you can break the chains of their enslavement.

OTHERS CAN TELL YOU THE TRUTH ABOUT HOW A PERSON IS KEEPING YOU FROM YOUR GOD-GIVEN PURPOSE AND CALLING IN LIFE, BUT ONLY YOU CAN BREAK THE CHAINS OF THEIR ENSLAVEMENT.

There is no need to waste time complaining about their unfair treatment of you: "I don't understand why they treat me this way! Why are they mean to me?" They treat you like trash because you let them! There is no point in pretending that they will change any time soon. Any change on their part will come about by the Lord dealing with them, and it helps when you and others stand up and refuse to buy the garbage they are peddling.

HONOR OR WORSHIP?

You can't break free from demonic control by becoming a controller yourself. The Bible teaches that you should *"Give everyone what you owe him...if respect, then respect; if honor, then honor"* (Romans 13:7). You can't break free by dishonoring the position people hold in your life. You should always honor your parents; you should always revere your pastor; and you should always respect officeholders. However, there is a vast difference between *respect* and *worship*. Worship is reserved only for God. Worship is unconditional surrender to serve. No human deserves your "unconditional" obedience. Obedience is good, but never at the expense of obeying God.

Satan tried to get Jesus to bow down to him, but Jesus replied, *"Away from me, Satan! For it is written: 'Worship the Lord your God, and serve him only.'"* (Matthew 4:10). Satan will indirectly try to get you to worship him by making you bow down to his servants who try to control you. Jesus said, *"Serve* [God] *only."*

God is the Maker. A potter has the right to do with the pottery what he desires. God is the Potter. He has the right, as your Maker, to do with you as He wants. God will not use you as an ashtray if you live for Him. He will make you an *"instrument for noble purposes"* (2 Timothy 2:21). While God will dignify you with a noble purpose, controllers only want to humiliate and use you.

Do others humiliate you? Do they do it to control you by making you feel unworthy to serve the Lord in a dignified way? Then remember that the Lord brings dignity to you. If a leader does not bring dignity to you, then something is desperately wrong!

If you let controllers put you down, it could be that you have bowed down to them. That is why you feel like a doormat. Get up! Stop bowing down to them. You are inadvertently worshipping them. You do not think you are, but if you let them control you, you are.

You can break free, not by being disrespectful for the office they hold, but by refusing to let them dictate your life. In some cases, you have to leave them! Of course, children, no matter how old they get, should never abandon their parents, and vice versa. Certainly there are instances in which children who have suffered abuse from a parent must erect boundaries to break the cycle of harmful control. Spouses should not divorce unless they have biblical grounds, such as abuse or adultery. (See 1 Corinthians 7:15; Matthew 19:9.) Also, there are undying ministerial relationships. While you should not abandon those "permanent" relationships without just cause, not all friendships and ministerial alliances are unending. When people hold temporary offices in your life, you are not bound to always stay with them. You can leave! And in some cases, you should! (I will address this more in chapter 4.)

CHARACTERISTICS OF CONTROLLERS

Jesus was so concerned about His own apostles misusing their authority that He gave them this instruction:

> *The kings of the Gentiles lord it over them; and those who exercise authority over them call themselves Benefactors. But you are not to be like that. Instead, the greatest among you should be like the youngest, and the one who rules like the one who serves.* (Luke 22:25–26)

Jesus used the phrase, "*lord it over them.*" He was saying to His disciples, "Do not play God."

This reminds me of two boys arguing as to which one was going to get the last pancake. The mother stopped the boys from arguing, asking, "Boys, what would Jesus do?" The oldest boy looked at his young brother and said to him, "You play Jesus!"

People playing God is no laughing matter. There are husbands who want to be god in the eyes of their wives. Controllers are not always those in an office of authority. Sometimes they are people who should submit to authority themselves—sometimes in the home, it is the wife who wields ungodly control, causing problems and even abuse. Pastors can try to play god, but sometimes members can, too. Bosses can play god, but so can employees. My point is this: no one, including those in offices and those under offices, should "lord" anything over others. Only God has the right to be Lord!

Those who misuse their authority *"call themselves Benefactors."* A *benefactor* is someone who bestows benefits to others. Jesus did not say they *were* benefactors, only that they *"call themselves"* by this title. I think Jesus was saying that they really do not benefit anyone—the only beneficiaries are themselves. That is how you can tell a real leader from a false one. Real leaders lead for the benefit of those who are following them. False leaders are only out there for themselves.

This is ultimately the sign of a controller: if a person is benefiting from your relationship, yet you are losing from the relationship, then they are a controller, not a good friend. Break free from controlling people. Stop letting others control you. In the next chapter, we will look at the five common kinds of manipulation that controlling people use.

THREE

HOW TO AVOID MANIPULATION

One of the dominant themes of the Bible is God's desire to free people from slavery. "*Therefore, say to the Israelites: 'I am the* L*ORD*, *and I will bring you out from under the yoke of the Egyptians. I will free you from being slaves to them, and I will redeem you with an outstretched arm and with mighty acts of judgment*'" (Exodus 6:6).

The main festival for the Jews is Passover. It is a celebration of the Israelites' freedom from the yoke of the Egyptians. Although we have lost sight of it over the centuries, today we know the truth: no one has the right to own slaves. Even the apostle Paul told Christians who lived in the Roman Empire that sanctioned slavery, "*Were you a slave when you were called? Don't let it trouble you—although if you can gain your freedom, do so"* (1 Corinthians 7:21). And for those Christian slaves who were bound in government-sanctioned slavery, Paul said, *"He who was a slave when he was called by the Lord is the Lord's freedman"* (verse 22).

This shows that it is possible to be in a binding relationship yet walk in freedom. Don't be so quick to think your only freedom is to divorce, to cut off ties with your parents, or to disown your children. You don't necessarily have to quit your job or end your membership at your church. So long as you walk in freedom, you can enjoy and make the best of any relationship. But to enjoy your relationships, you will have to learn to stop allowing yourself to be so easily manipulated.

FIVE KINDS OF MANIPULATIONS

There are five basic ways in which people can try to manipulate you. Don't let them.

1. EMOTIONAL MANIPULATION

This is the most common manipulation that people try to employ. A wife might cry to her husband, "You don't love me!"

A husband, on the other hand, might use anger: "I am going to walk out if you don't give me what I want!"

Silence can be a deafening form of manipulation. When my wife and I were newlyweds, we were young and childish. One night, we got into an argument, and neither of us would budge. So we went to sleep together, or, at least, we feigned sleep. We broke the Scripture that says, *"Do not let the sun go down while you are still angry"* (Ephesians 4:26).

Sonia lay on her right side; I lay on my left. Silence. I could not sleep, but I didn't want to give her the satisfaction of knowing she had robbed me of my sleep, so I pretended to—I even gave it a little fake snore. When I did, she let out a little whimper of a cry. Still no budging. Finally, Sonia could take the silence no longer; she let out a loud cry.

I responded, "Why did you wake me?"

Yeah, right! Well, we made up. But here's the point: my silence was a form of manipulation. When someone tries the silent treatment on you, keep the lines of communication open, even if they refuse to respond. Don't imitate them. If your parents don't want to talk to you, still talk to them. Call them. If they hang up, try later. On Mother's Day and Father's Day, send them a card. Wish them a happy birthday. Don't give up.

WHEN SOMEONE TRIES THE SILENT TREATMENT ON YOU, KEEP THE LINES OF COMMUNICATION OPEN, EVEN IF THEY REFUSE TO RESPOND. DON'T IMITATE THEM.

You say, "I can't do that. I feel like they are gaining pleasure in my constant reaching out to them." But Jesus said, *"If someone strikes you on one cheek, turn to him the other also"* (Luke 6:29). By doing so, you turn the tables. You make the other person feel guilty over their meanness to you. Don't fight fire with fire. That's stupid, because you will just get a bigger fire.

If you play with them using the silent treatment, you only torment yourself and prolong the problem in your relationship. Be honest, do you really have fun being angry and not communicating with the person you love? Of course not, it's a miserable feeling. Stop making yourself miserable; let the other person be miserable. Make them feel badly for mistreating you. How? By you being the opposite. You be nice. You speak kindly.

The apostle Paul had advice for slaves who were being mistreated: *"Serve wholeheartedly, as if you were serving the Lord, not men, because you know that the Lord will reward everyone for whatever good he does, whether he is slave or free"* (Ephesians 6:7–8). God's eye is on you, and so is His reward. *"If your enemy is hungry, give him food to eat; if he is thirsty, give him water to drink. In doing this, you will heap burning coals on his head, and the Lord will reward you"* (Proverbs 25:21–22).

Two things are accomplished when you take the high road in any relationship: First, by doing good to those that don't deserve it, you *"heap burning coals"* on their heads. This means you make them feel guilty over their mistreatment of you. You might argue, "This person will never feel guilty." Maybe so, but the second benefit is guaranteed: *"The Lord will reward you."*

In most cases, both blessings will take place in your life. You will win over the enemy and you will be rewarded by God.

2. CRITICAL MANIPULATION

Goliath tried this on David: *"He said to David, 'Am I a dog, that you come at me with sticks?' And the Philistine cursed David by his gods"* (1 Samuel 17:43). People will curse you with their words. Don't be afraid of their cursing, because God will turn their cursing into a boomerang.

Don't let their words penetrate your spirit. Don't let them defile your faith. Believe in God's love for you. Believe that God is on your side. Say out loud, *"The Lord is on my side"* (Psalm 118:6 ESV).

David, in his own words, said just this. He knew God was on the side of His covenant people. He answered back,

> *You come against me with sword and spear and javelin, but I come against you in the name of the* Lord *Almighty, the God of the armies of Israel, whom you have defied.... All those gathered here will know that it is not by sword or spear that the* Lord *saves; for the battle is the* Lord*'s, and he will give all of you into our hands.* (1 Samuel 17:45, 47)

David did not brag on himself, he boasted in the Lord his God. When people criticize you, say what the Word of God says about you. When they condemn you for your past, speak back, "The Lord has forgiven me." When they predict that your life will not amount to anything, answer back, "God has plans to prosper me and not to harm me, plans to give me hope and a future." (See Jeremiah 29:11.)

CRITICISM IS MEANT TO MAKE YOU FEEL GUILTY, POWERLESS, AND HOPELESS. YOU CAN'T FEEL THIS WAY. YOU WILL BE A SLAVE TO FEAR IF YOU SUCCUMB TO UNJUST AND MEAN CRITICISM. STAY STRONG IN THE LORD!

Don't answer in the flesh; answer in the Spirit. Say what God says about you, and stop putting yourself down. There are enough people who will try to put you down; don't cooperate with them. Criticism is meant to make you feel guilty, powerless, and hopeless. You can't feel this way. You will be a slave to fear if you succumb to unjust and mean criticism. Stay strong in the Lord!

3. FINANCIAL MANIPULATION

God's answer to people who threaten you by withholding money from you is found in Philippians 4:19: *"And my God will meet all your needs according to his glorious riches in Christ Jesus."*

Do not make people your source of blessings—people, at best, can only be a channel of blessings. The source, however, is God! If a channel of money threatens to stop providing money to you, then trust God for another channel.

A former member of my church tried to manipulate us financially. We were very small at the beginning and depended a lot on each family. My wife was the treasurer, and knew what each family was giving. This member made it clear to me that there were some subjects of the Bible that he preferred to hear preached on more than other subjects. When I would preach on the subjects he did not like, he did not give in the offering. This was a form of financial manipulation. Many pastors with struggling budgets may feel the strong pull to preach in a way that doesn't ruffle any feathers. But you can't give in. You cannot allow people to scare you. I know you need money to live, but you don't need one single person to be the channel of blessings.

Elijah was fed by a raven, but eventually, the brook dried up and the raven stopped feeding Elijah. Yet, God had another channel of blessing—an unexpected one. A widow was the next channel of blessing to Elijah. (See 1 Kings 17:7–16.) Even when one channel dried up, Elijah trusted in God's provision, just as we should do.

4. PHYSICAL MANIPULATION

This form can come through abuse, neglect, or even sex. In some cases, physical manipulation crosses the line and becomes a crime. If someone commits a crime against you, report it. Don't let anyone get away with physically hurting you.

There are some disagreements within the church as to whether or not physical abuse is grounds for separation and divorce. I believe it is based on Malachi 2:16: "'*The man who hates and divorces his wife,' says the* LORD, *the God of Israel, 'does violence to the one he should protect,' says the* LORD *Almighty*" (Malachi 2:16 NIV11). God puts divorce on the same level as physical violence. In fact, He shames the divorcing husband by saying that his action does "*violence*" to his wife. In other words, it appears that violence is a greater evil than divorce.

Someone might argue, "Jesus never said that physical violence was a condition for divorce." Jesus did not have to, because violence against a woman was considered the most cowardly action of a man. When a husband hit his wife, it put the wife above the husband. It gave her, with the sanction of the community, the right to leave the man. No one under the old covenant could injure another. Even a master was punished for injuring his slave. There could be nothing worse than a husband who physically abused his wife. Don't let anyone abuse you.

My wife and I were asked to visit a lady who had recently started coming to our church. We went to her house, and she told us, "I am confused. I use to go another church with my husband, but he got arrested for sexually molesting our daughter. The pastor said that I could not divorce him because he did not commit adultery. He told me that when he gets out of prison, I have to take him back. What do you think?"

My blood was boiling when I heard this. I told her, "That pastor is completely wrong! You cannot put your daughter at risk with this man. You have every right to divorce him. You need to get as far away from him as possible."

Another form of physical manipulation is abandonment. A husband or wife leaves, a parent walks out on the children—this is physical manipulation, and it cannot be tolerated. A father who walks out on his family must be taken to court to pay child support. Wives, you cannot let your children suffer because their father abandoned them. The apostle Paul considered abandonment to be equal to divorce: *"If the unbelieving partner separates, let it be so. In such cases the brother or sister is not enslaved. God has called you to peace"* (1 Corinthians 7:15 ESV).

The answer to someone wanting to leave you is *"let it be so."* Don't beg them to stay. Don't hang on to their leg while they drag you out with them—let them go! No one is so important that you cannot live without them. Stop any thinking that makes you a slave to the person who does not want to be with you.

Show dignity to yourself. You are more important than that. Don't be in bondage to anyone. If a person threatens you with leaving, but they don't want to go, then they will see your strength. They won't be trying that again.

Yet another form of physical manipulation is withholding sex. No spouse has the right to withhold sex, unless they are obviously sick.

> *The husband should fulfill his marital duty to his wife, and likewise the wife to her husband. The wife's body does not belong to her alone but also to her husband. In the same way, the husband's body does not belong to him alone but also to his wife. Do not deprive each other except by mutual consent and for a time, so that you may devote yourselves to prayer. Then come together again so that Satan will not tempt you because of your lack of self-control.*
>
> (1 Corinthians 7:3–5)

The unique relation that husbands and wives have is sex. No one else has that relationship with them. So to deprive your spouse of sex is stealing from him or her. Your spouse should not refuse sex with you. The answer is not to force your spouse. That is wrong, and besides, you don't want to have sex with someone who does not want to willingly give it to you out of love.

Rather, if a spouse is withholding for wrong reasons, the answer at that point is counseling, and couples should get help quickly. No good Christian pastor or counselor will agree with your spouse who is withholding affection. He or she is trying to manipulate you to get what they want. You can't give in to this manipulation.

5. SPIRITUAL MANIPULATION

Cults use manipulation all the time. They try to make you feel that if you leave their group or religion, you are disobeying God or some other form of deity. They use fear to keep you in bondage. Don't let them. If you are part of a cult, get out quickly. Don't even talk to the leader. Run!

IT IS NOT JUST CULTS THAT USE SPIRITUAL MANIPULATION. EVEN CHRISTIANS AND CHURCHES CAN USE IT.

It is not just cults that use spiritual manipulation. Even Christians and churches can use it. A prophetess tried to control the wife of a famous evangelist. She convinced the wife to leave her husband. Even though there were no scriptural grounds for the divorce, the wife divorced him anyway.

The husband tried, on numerous occasions, to talk to his wife, but the prophetess would not allow it. She even gave words, supposedly coming from God, to the wife. This put the wife in bondage to the prophetess and ruined the marriage. Eventually, the wife broke free from this ungodly soul tie with the prophetess and remarried her husband.

Many Christians are under bondage from supposedly spiritual people. My members sometimes ask me, "Bishop, what do you think about this minister telling people to give a certain amount of money, and that if they do, God will heal them or do some miracle for them?"

I tell them that God promises to bless generosity, but you shouldn't be compelled to give out of fear. God will bless the tither, and that you can count on, but you don't have to give to one particular minister, especially if you are compelled out of fear.

The Bible says, *"Each man should give what he has decided in his heart to give, not reluctantly or under compulsion, for God loves a cheerful giver"* (2 Corinthians 9:7). You determine the amount to give. Don't be forced into giving a certain amount, thinking God won't bless you if you give less. Anyone preaching this message is trying to manipulate you. The Bible says give what you have decided in your heart to give. The amount is up to you. Second, don't give under compulsion; compulsion is a form of manipulation. Don't be manipulated to give, but rather give out of joy, and be cheerful when you give. Of course, I am not implying that you don't need to tithe. Tithing is scriptural and is taught by Jesus Christ Himself in Matthew 23:23. God will bless you if you tithe. I am saying you don't need to tithe to spiritual manipulators who are trying to make you give unscripturally to them.

Another form of spiritual manipulation is misuse of spiritual gifts. God can give visions to people, but the devil can also give them counterfeit visions. This is why the Bible says, *"Do not quench the Spirit. Do not despise prophecies, but test everything; hold fast what is good"* (1 Thessalonians 5:19–21 ESV). You don't want to be skeptical of the supernatural, but you also don't want to be gullible. Test everything.

If a person claims to have a vision or a word from God that benefits them, then I would be very skeptical. If it benefits only them and not others, it is likely a form of control. Don't let people put you under such bondage.

A man once came to my church and said, "God told me that He will take away your ministry in two years."

I laughed, and told him, "You are liar."

He swore that God told him this.

I said, "Now, in two years, if this does not come true, will you come to me personally to apologize?"

He agreed.

That was more than fifteen years ago; the church is now bigger than ever before. I am still waiting for his apology. I don't let people manipulate me with negative prophecies. They don't scare me!

You must have a backbone. Don't let scary visions, dreams, or prophecies frighten you. Stand strong in God's written Word. Know His promises to you!

FOUR

FOUR LEVELS OF AUTHORITY

The doctrine of submission has been abused by many leaders. As I pointed out in a previous chapter, Jesus warned His disciples about misusing their authority. The hardest soul tie to break free from is the tie with those who have authority over you. This chapter is important because once you understand the different levels of authority in your life, you will be able to discern which one has authority over you at any given time.

For example, your boss, your spouse, your parents, your pastor, your mayor, and others have certain levels of authority over your life. You don't want to be rebellious, but at the same time, you don't want to be demonically controlled by a corrupt authority figure, either.

It is true that the Bible teaches submission to authority, but it also informs us that not all levels of authority are equal. And these different levels of authority require different levels of submission. A higher authority always overrules a lower authority. It's similar to a court system, in which there are county courts, then state courts, then federal courts, and finally the Supreme Court. Higher courts can overturn the lower courts. The same is true with levels of authority. There are different levels of authority in your life, and you must be aware of each one. When the authorities contradict each other, you must obey the higher authority.

Negative soul ties are developed when you serve the lower authority at the expense of disobeying the higher authority in your life.

Here are the four vital levels of authority in your life:

1. THE AUTHORITY OF GOD

The highest level of authority is God. All human authority is derived from Him. The Bible says, *"Everyone must submit to the governing authorities, for there is no authority except that which God has established. The authorities that exist have been established by God"* (Romans 13:1).

All *"governing authorities"* derive their authority from One greater than themselves—God! This is why they are called *delegated* authorities. Delegated authorities derive their authority from God, which makes them subservient to Him. The only authority they have has been given to them by God. No one can make you submit to them while making you disobey God. That kind of authority is not divine, but demonic.

On the other hand, God never received authority from anyone. He is the architect of authority. Authority began in Him and His authority is *sovereign* authority. No one but God has sovereign authority. Sovereign authority can never be disputed. If you don't like what God tells you to do—too bad! You must obey without question. You don't have a right to argue with God's commands. They stem from His sovereign authority.

No one can demand your obedience in the exact same way that God can, and that includes your parents, spouse, minister, teacher, boss, president, and everyone else. Their authority is given by God, so how can they demand that you disobey the source of their authority?

> *Now I want you to realize that the head of every man is Christ, and the head of the woman is man, and the head of Christ is God.* (1 Corinthians 11:3)

Clearly, levels of authority are mentioned here. Paul affirms the idea that husbands are the head of their wives, but that Christ is the head of the husband. And eventually, even God, the Father, is the head of Christ, the Son.

How does this headship work? It is quite simple. Wives should respectfully *"submit to* [their] *husbands as to the Lord"* (Ephesians 5:22). Even so, a wife is not ordered to obey any expectation from the husband that does not line up with the teachings of Jesus Christ. Jesus Christ is the head of the husband, so if the husband gets out of line, the wife does not have to get in line behind her husband. Instead, she is permitted to disobey her husband if it means obeying Christ. Christ is her higher authority, and she will only develop a negative soul tie if she obeys the lower authority, her husband, instead of her higher authority.

Angie told me that her husband does not want her to come to my church. I asked her, "What church does your husband attend?" She said that he sometimes went to a particular church that really did not teach the full gospel. In addition, he didn't even attend very often.

I advised her, "Angie, talk to your husband. Tell him how much you respect him, and that in every way you can, you will follow him. But when it comes to church, tell him that you will continue going to Bishop Tom's church, where you feel you can learn the full gospel." She did this. Her boldness and respect touched her husband. He now loves coming to my church, too.

The idea of submission is contrary to the world's disrespectful attitude. It seems that we live in an honorless society, at least in America. Many people are very disrespectful to authority.

Perhaps submission is so negatively viewed because people misinterpret its meaning. Maybe people think it means to be a doormat. It does not! Maybe they think submission means the person in authority is better than they are. They are not! Submission to authority does not imply an inequality in the human race, only that some people are placed in genuine places of authority. All people are equal; some people have more authority in certain areas than others.

Notice that Paul said, *"the head of Christ is God."* Yet Christ is indeed God—God the Son. As an obedient Son, however, He submits to His heavenly Father. Jesus said, *"The Father is greater than I"* (John 14:28). Jesus did not say that the Father is "better" than I. The words *better* and *greater* mean different things. *Better* is a reference to quality. *Greater* is a reference to authority. Jesus and the Father are one! Jesus is God; He shares the very attributes of God the Father. But in terms of authority, the Father is higher than the Son.

This is a beautiful relationship. It shows that you can submit to human authority while still being equal to the authority. A wife is equal to her husband; submission doesn't make her less than he. The same is true of all relationships. Your parents are greater than you in that they gave you life, yet they share the same number of chromosomes as you do. You submit out of respect, not out of inferiority.

If you do feel inferior to someone else, it means that you are in a bad relationship with that person. It could be your fault that you feel inferior. In that case, you need to change your self-image. (I'll discuss this in the last section.) But when others intentionally try to make you feel inferior, then you need to break that soul tie. Don't allow that to happen!

WHEN OTHERS INTENTIONALLY TRY TO MAKE YOU FEEL INFERIOR, THEN YOU NEED TO BREAK THAT SOUL TIE. DON'T ALLOW THAT TO HAPPEN!

No one should demand unconditional obedience. To every human, Christ is the ultimate head, even if they are not aware of it. Good leaders are ever conscious of Christ's authority over them.

Every human authority is accountable to God's authority. For example, Peter and John were forbidden to preach by the religious authorities. What was their response? *"But Peter and John replied, 'Judge for yourselves whether it is right in God's sight to obey you rather than God.'"* (Acts 4:19). Peter and John differentiated between sovereign authority and delegated authority. They always respected the Sanhedrin, but they could not allow the Sanhedrin's orders to go against Christ's orders to preach the gospel to the whole world.

Whenever delegated authority demands something other than what God demands, you must disobey them and submit to God's authority. To do otherwise is to rebel against sovereign authority. Atrocities have been permitted because people obeyed delegated authorities instead of sovereign authority. Think of Germany during the Holocaust. Cults have been formed because people obeyed religious dictators instead of God. Spousal abuse is often exacerbated because women were told to submit to their malevolent husbands.

However, whenever delegated authorities do not demand that you to disobey God, they should be obeyed. You do not have to *accept* every decision that delegated authorities make, but unless they compel you to disobey God, then you *respect* their decisions.

For example, the US Supreme Court ruled that homosexuals have a constitutional right to get married. Now, there is nothing I can do about this terrible decision. But if the government insists that I, or my church, act in a way that is contrary to God's commands, then the government has become tyrannical. I would have no choice but to disobey them!

IF THE GOVERNMENT INSISTS THAT I, OR MY CHURCH, ACT IN A WAY THAT IS CONTRARY TO GOD'S COMMANDS, THEN THE GOVERNMENT HAS BECOME TYRANNICAL. I WOULD HAVE NO CHOICE BUT TO DISOBEY THEM!

Similarly, delegated authority (our government) permits the evil of abortion, but, they don't impose this evil on anyone. No one is forced to get abortions, as is the case in China. Since the government does not impose abortion, we cannot rebel against the government in this case.

Now, when the government demands that Christian-owned businesses provide healthcare that supports life-killing procedures, then they have become tyrannical. It is one thing for them to legalize this evil, but it's another thing to force others to contribute to it or participate in it.

I bring up these two social cases to explain that so long as those in authority do not force me to go against Christ, I cannot rebel against the government. I can only disobey the government when they demand that I or my church go against Christ.

You cannot force others to agree with your viewpoints. You cannot, for example, break the law by trespassing on abortion clinics. You cannot force women not to get an abortion. You also cannot stop homosexuals from getting married in their own way.

In the same way, you cannot rebel against your husband or your pastor because you disagree with their decisions. So long as they are not directly ordering you to disobey God, then you should respect their decisions.

2. THE AUTHORITY OF TRUTH

Jesus said, *"I am the way and the truth and the life"* (John 14:6).

This brings us to an important point: How do you know whether or not delegated authority is requiring something of you that is contradictory to God's commands? How do you know whether they have overridden their authority?

The answer is simple: In order to protect you, God has made known to you His commands. The Bible is the sole authority for your life. So in a practical sense, you live by the authority of truth. If something is true, it doesn't matter what any other authority has to say. Truth overrides all delegated authority.

THE BIBLE IS THE SOLE AUTHORITY FOR YOUR LIFE. SO IN A PRACTICAL SENSE, YOU LIVE BY THE AUTHORITY OF TRUTH. IF SOMETHING IS TRUE, IT DOESN'T MATTER WHAT ANY OTHER AUTHORITY HAS TO SAY. TRUTH OVERRIDES ALL DELEGATED AUTHORITY.

When Christ walked the earth, He always affirmed the Holy Scriptures. When debating with Pharisees and Sadducees, Jesus would appeal to the Word of God. He often said, *"Haven't you read...?"* For example, when the religious leaders condemned Jesus' disciples for plucking grain and eating it on the Sabbath, Jesus pointed out that the Bible says that David ate consecrated bread. By appealing to the scriptural account of David, Jesus showed there is nothing wrong with eating on the Sabbath. Bread is holy and yet edible to God! (See Matthew 12:1–8.)

Jesus pointed to Scriptures as the source of authority. Now Jesus was Himself the personification of the Word of God, yet He made His appeal to the written Word of God. The application for your life is simple: no matter what others teach, and no matter what laws are made, the Scriptures are the truth.

The Supreme Court says that men may marry men and women marry women, but the Word of God teaches that God made man and woman to marry each other. Jesus said:

> *"Haven't you read," he replied, "that at the beginning the Creator 'made them male and female,' and said, 'For this reason a man will leave his father and mother and be united to his wife, and the two will become one flesh'? So they are no longer two, but one flesh. Therefore what God has joined together, let no one separate."* (Matthew 19:4–6)

If a minister says that he is going to marry homosexuals, he is wrong in the light of Scripture. He may have been ordained and approved by others, but he is disapproved of by God. If you belong to a church that sanctions this immorality, you are under no obligation to stay. By leaving, you are not rebelling against authority, but submitting to God's authority. Apply this principle in all your relationships! If you do, you will keep ungodly soul ties from forming in your life.

3. THE AUTHORITY OF YOUR CONSCIENCE

There will always be debatable gray areas. The Bible is not always black and white in every moral or practical issue.

For example, the Word of God commands you to preach the gospel to every creature. Let's say you feel God has called you to preach full-time. You go to your pastor, and ask him to ordain you. Your pastor says, "No, wait and submit." Now what do you do? He did not say you cannot be ordained; he was just not ready to ordain you because he felt you were not ready. You, however, feel that you are ready! You both disagree. You don't have a particular verse to *prove* you are ready, but you *feel* that you are ready. This is where the conscience plays a role in authority. Eventually, conscience will play a part in guiding you.

Where does God say to wait first before you preach? He said to the disciples to wait in Jerusalem until they were endued with power from on high. Once they were endued with the power of the Holy Spirit, Jesus said, "*Go into all the world and preach the good news to all creation*" (Mark 16:15).

When you are interpreting the Bible differently from those in authority then you must go by your conscience. This is called the "authority of the conscience." Paul writes: "*Therefore, it is necessary to submit to the authorities, not only because of possible punishment but also as a matter of conscience*" (Romans 13:5).

Conscience plays a high role in authority. Whenever a person transgresses his conscience, then he or she has sinned. The conscience is given to us as a judge to decide between debatable matters. Debatable matters include whether or not to participate in drinking or dancing, what movies to see, or what clothes to wear. The Bible does not give specific guidelines for these matters. However, it does give specific commands for matters like drunkenness, lewdness, pornography, and immodesty. These are not up for debate.

If someone requires you to go against your conscience, they are not acting righteously. Don't be under bondage to them. You can still respect them, but you must follow your conscience.

4. THE AUTHORITY OF PEOPLE

> *Children, obey your parents in the Lord, for this is right.*
> (Ephesians 6:1)

> *Everyone must submit himself to the governing authorities, for there is no authority except that which God has established.* (Romans 13:1)

> *Obey your leaders and submit to their authority.*
> (Hebrews 13:17)

There would be no order and structure without God delegating authority to various people in your life. The Bible does not cover everything commanded by God. For example, what times should a child come home from a party? If a child gets bad grades, what should be the discipline? There is nothing in the Bible to tell a parent what to do in those cases. Parent's use their own discretion to decide these things for their children. If parents did not have this authority, children would grow up without the needed discipline to be successful in their lives.

ONLY GOD IS SOVEREIGN; HE RULES WITHOUT BEING ACCOUNTABLE TO ANYONE ELSE. ALL HUMAN AUTHORITY IS ACCOUNTABLE TO GOD.

For another example, the Ten Commandments do not cover zoning laws, speed limits, and various ordinances necessary to run a city, state, or country. You cannot find anything in the Bible to cover most of the laws that governments must institute for law and order. So God put humans in charge of governing people. Without government, everyone would do what is right in their own eyes, and the result would be chaos.

Similarly, concerning the church, God's Word does not cover issues of budgets, guest speakers, and other issues of governance. In the absence of scriptural mandate, church leaders and ruling denominations should make those decisions for the congregation. As a member of the church, you must accept, obey, and submit to those decisions.

Human authority, therefore, gets its authority from God. This means human authority derives its authority from God's sovereignty. Only God is sovereign; He rules without being accountable to anyone else. All human authority is accountable to God.

In a practical way, you must obey human authority so long as that human authority is submitted to God's sovereign authority. Ungodly soul ties are created when a human authority expects you to submit to them in the same manner as you would submit to God. Only God can demand unconditional submission.

So long as human authority respects the authority of God, the authority of truth, and the authority of your conscience, then human authority becomes a blessing.

Unfortunately, in America, government is increasingly disrespecting God, truth, and human conscience. As I stated before, when the federal government forces business owners to participate in funding abortion for their employees or forces them to provide goods and services for homosexual weddings, this becomes tyranny.

Having suffered under the tyrannical government of the king of England, our founding fathers were well aware of the potential dangers inherent in government. Thus, they made sure that their new government would remain small, and that greater power would be granted to governmental entities closer to the people, such as municipalities, cities, and states. Fewer powers for the federal government meant less fear of their abuse.

They also divided the powers of the federal government into three different branches. They did not want an American king to have executive, legislative, and judicial powers, as kings so often did in other nations. Instead, they created the office of the presidency and gave him or her only executive powers. Legislative power, the power of making laws, was given to the

Congress, which was deemed to be closer to the people. Finally, they gave judicial powers to the Supreme Court. Only the judicial branch is appointed, not elected, in an effort to prevent decisions based on the will of the people rather than the rule of law.

These three branches spring from Isaiah 33:22: *"For the Lord is our judge, the Lord is our lawgiver, the Lord is our king; it is he who will save us."* Only God is sovereign and sits in all three branches. The founding fathers had the wisdom to restrict human power to a bare minimum. This resulted in the formation of the greatest nation in human history.

Today, the founding principles of limited government are being challenged by those who want a stronger federal government. They want to impose a version of morality onto our citizens. In my opinion, Supreme Court justices have failed to uphold the constitution in certain important cases. The Tenth Amendment grants all powers to the states that are not specifically granted to the federal government, yet the Supreme Court has forced states to dismantle their abortion and marriage laws. In such cases, the states are ceding more and more power to the federal government. I believe that if this trend is not reversed, it will be the undoing of the great democratic experiment that built this country.

DEGREES OF AUTHORITY

The best human authority is always found in the authority that is the most local. But this authority will change over time. After birth, parents have a greater authority over their children than any other human authority can have. Then, the authority of humans lessens as you grow older and become more independent. For many, the next level of authority over your life will be teachers. They do not have as great an authority as your parents had, but their authority is still significant. Eventually, the next level of authority in your life will be a boss. Then you get married and you have another person you are accountable to. As a wife, you are told in the Bible to submit to your husband. This may be hard to do. As a husband, you are commanded to sacrifice for your wife as Christ sacrificed for His bride, the church. This is even harder to do than to submit. Yet, the wife is not a child. The husband does not have authority over the wife in the same way as he would over his children. The degree of authority is different.

AS YOU GROW OLDER, THE AUTHORITY PEOPLE HAVE OVER YOUR LIFE SHOULD DECREASE. THE OLDER YOU GET, THE MORE GOD SHOULD DIRECTLY RULE IN YOUR LIFE. HOWEVER, UNGODLY SOUL TIES KEEP YOU FROM BECOMING MORE DEPENDENT ON GOD.

Bad soul ties are developed when a husband forgets that his level of authority over his wife is much less than that of a parent over a child, because she is far more independent. You cannot develop good relationships if you continue to submit as a child. As an adult, the authority of others over your life is simply not as great as it was when you were a child.

Marriage requires submission, but not the same degree as children submit to parents. You should not treat your spouse as a child, nor should you allow anyone to treat you as a child.

A parent can stop a child from seeing a friend; a spouse cannot demand that a husband or wife stop seeing a friend. A parent decides what food the child will eat, what church the child will go to, and what financial allowance the child gets, but not so with spouses.

As you grow older, the authority people have over your life should decrease. The older you get, the more God should directly rule in your life. However, ungodly soul ties keep you from becoming more dependent on God. This is bad! It is not God's plan.

Jennifer was a devoted young adult in her church. She was the piano player. Yet, her emotional development was stunted. She did not grow up with the same confidence that most people develop as they get older.

Once, when a visiting evangelist talked to her, she immediately went into a shell. She could not even make eye contact with him because she was so shy. The evangelist asked the pastor about her, and was told that the woman had a dominant mother. The pastor pointed out the mother in the congregation.

Later, the mother came up to the evangelist, and asked if he could pray for her daughter. She said, "I am very concerned for my daughter. There are boys that like her. I am concerned she is going to leave me and get involved with a boy. So please pray that my daughter stays with me and doesn't go out with a boy."

The evangelist responded, "Did you raise your daughter with good values?"

"Yes, of course."

"Does she love the Lord?"

"Absolutely! Why are you asking me these questions?"

In a stern voice, the evangelist said, "It's because your daughter is emotionally stunted. You have put her under your thumb.

It is not right to keep your daughter scared of the world. Yes, we are not of the world, but we have to live in it. She is afraid, and you have made her afraid. I am not going to pray that your daughter stays at home; I am going to pray that she gets out of your house and lives on her own."

The mother was at first upset, but the conviction that she had done wrong hit her. She eventually released her daughter to God. The evangelist encouraged the mother to release the chains of authority, and the daughter greatly improved, gained confidence, and eventually married a good man.

The same principles hold for relationships with pastors and spiritual leaders as well. At first, when you become a born-again Christian and join the church, the pastor will have greater influence over your life. As you grow more in the Lord, his or her influence should grow less. An ungodly soul tie develops when the pastor insists that you become more and more dependent on him instead of less and less. You need to break that increasing dependence!

Sometimes, this increasing dependence is not the pastor's fault. Sometimes, it's because of your own insecurity that you grow more dependent on him. You may even become a "fan" or "groupie" of his or her ministry. I have seen this happen so often and it's not healthy!

God has given you more than one person to help grow you in the Lord. Paul wrote, *"For when one says, 'I follow Paul,' and another, 'I follow Apollos,' are you not mere men?"* (1 Corinthians 3:4). Paul calls them not just mere men but *"mere infants in Christ"* (verse 1). An infant is totally dependent on parents. Paul was saying that as you grow up in Christ, you should wean yourself off of your initial spiritual parents and learn from others. He concludes by writing, *"All things are yours, whether Paul or*

Apollos or Cephas or the world or life or death or the present or the future—all are yours" (1 Corinthians 3:21–22).

Spiritual parents are important—always respect and listen to them. But as you grow, open up your horizon and see that there are more ministers to learn from.

Sylvia was a good member. Yet she became a groupie of a famous evangelist. All she could talk about was this minister. She rarely mentioned any teacher except him.

I noticed that her spiritual growth was stunted. To this day, her testimony has been hurt by her ungodly soul tie. Now, the minister was completely unaware of this woman's infatuation with him. It was not his fault, it was hers.

How about you? As you grow in Christ, are you learning to become more dependent on God and less dependent on other humans? You should! If you haven't, then brace yourself as we embark on the causes of bad soul ties!

PART II
SOUL TIES

FIVE

WHAT IS A GOOD SOUL TIE?

You cannot know what a devilish soul tie is until you contrast it with a godly soul tie. David and Jonathan are great examples of a good, godly soul tie. Listen to what the Bible says about them:

> *And it came to pass, when he had made an end of speaking unto Saul, that the soul of Jonathan was knit with the soul of David, and Jonathan loved him as his own soul. And Saul took him that day, and would let him go no more home to his father's house. Then Jonathan and David made a covenant, because he loved him as his own soul. And Jonathan stripped himself of the robe that was upon him, and gave it to David, and his garments, even to his sword, and to his bow, and to his girdle.* (1 Samuel 18:1–4 KJV)

The Bible says that the *"soul of Jonathan was knit with the soul of David."* A good soul tie is an emotional connection based on true friendship. David's relationship with Jonathan blessed him. It even protected him from an untimely death. Good soul ties are meant to bless you. Relationships should be a great blessing.

Wise Solomon wrote, *"If either of them falls down, one can help the other up. But pity anyone who falls and has no one to help them up"* (Ecclesiastes 4:10). You will need help from someone; you cannot go it alone. You must have friends.

THE SOUL TIE BETWEEN JESUS AND JUDAS

Jesus needed friends, and so He had soul ties with twelve apostles. He was very close to them. Yet even Jesus had a bad soul tie with Judas. In describing Jesus' emotional feelings for Judas, David prophetically wrote, *"I once enjoyed sweet fellowship as we walked with the throng at the house of God"* (Psalm 55:14). Jesus was not distant with Judas, He was close to him. The relationship is described as *"sweet fellowship."* Jesus enjoyed His time with Judas. Yet, the soul tie came to hurt Jesus.

David wrote, *"If an enemy were insulting me, I could endure it; if a foe were raising himself against me, I could hide from him. But it is you, a man like myself, my companion, my close friend"* (verses 12–13). Don't gloss over the closeness Jesus felt with Judas. Judas is not described as an enemy. This is what made the betrayal so hurtful. If an enemy had betrayed Christ, then it would be easy to endure. But it was a *"close friend"* that did it.

According to Psalm 41:9, Judas was Jesus' best friend: *"My best and truest friend, who ate at my table, has even turned against me"* (NCV). They had meals together. They laughed together. They shared and talked with each other. They had a normal, healthy relationship. Yet, Judas betrayed their friendship. It is possible to have a good soul tie with someone, which then turns bad. Do not feel horrible if you have a friend who betrays you; it happened with your Lord, too.

How did the Lord handle betrayal? As the sound of marching soldiers drew near to the garden, Jesus spoke to the Eleven, *"Look, the hour is near, and the Son of Man is delivered into the hands of sinners. Rise, let us go! Here comes my betrayer!"* (Matthew 26:45–46). Jesus did not take the blame for Judas's action. He put Judas in the category of *"sinner"* and *"betrayer."* By doing so, Jesus separated Himself from Judas. He did not accept Judas as part of the holy apostles. Judas's sinful action separated him from the Twelve.

There is a moral lesson for you: once someone close to you has betrayed you, do not blame yourself or continue the relationship. Jesus ended the friendship because Judas dishonored it first. You must, too.

ONCE SOMEONE CLOSE TO YOU HAS BETRAYED YOU, DO NOT BLAME YOURSELF OR CONTINUE THE RELATIONSHIP. JESUS ENDED THE FRIENDSHIP BECAUSE JUDAS DISHONORED IT FIRST. YOU MUST, TOO.

I am not talking about ending relationships simply over disagreements, hurt feelings, arguments, or anything similar. What Judas did was not merely to disagree with the direction of Jesus' ministry, but to overthrow it! He might not have known that his action would put Jesus to death, but he certainly intended to put an end to Jesus' ministry. Make no mistake about it, Judas's action was betrayal.

The rest of the disciples hurt Christ, too, by denying Him. They were afraid, and did this to save their own lives. Christ understood! He forgave them and reaffirmed their calling in the holy apostleship.

You have to learn when a friend is acting to hurt you, and when he or she is acting because they are hurt. A true friend may hurt you unintentionally—you can forgive them and make up—but when a friend works to hurt you and stop your walk with God, then that is different. In those rare cases, you must break the soul tie.

The story continues. "[Judas] *approached Jesus to kiss him, but Jesus asked him, 'Judas, are you betraying the Son of Man with a kiss?'*" (Luke 22:47–48).

Jesus was not deceived by the apparent affection of Judas. He called him to account for pretending to love Him. Sometimes a betrayer will pretend they have your back, but they are actually hiding a knife. You must have discernment from the Holy Spirit to be able to catch Satan trying to ruin you through a fake friend.

The Bible says that Judas did kiss Jesus. There is another lesson: Jesus let him! He did not slap his face. You will never break soul ties by acting in the flesh. You must break them in the Spirit, which means that you must continue to walk in love! Your flesh will scream out for revenge: "How dare they do that to me?" Let it go. Jesus let it go. He knew the kiss was insincere, but He let Judas kiss Him anyway. It's best to let the betrayer leave with a kiss—not you kissing them, but them pretending to show affection and love to you.

Finally, Jesus knew this was all God's plan. The betrayal led to Jesus' trial, His sentence, and His crucifixion. But the crucifixion was for the benefit of the world. He died for us all! He also knew that death could not hold Him down. So it is with you. You cannot let the betrayal, the broken soul ties, hold you down. Do not keep grieving, because the betrayal will work for your good.

Jesus did not give up on the concept of apostleship. He did not rise from the dead and, in anger, say to all of His apostles, "I'm through with trying to build the church through men. I am ending your role as apostles. Judas hurt me; you hurt me. I'm through with it all!"

It is easy to feel so hurt that you don't want to have any more soul ties. Your marriage may have ended, so you are through with marriage. Someone in church hurt you, so you are through with church. Someone in your family hurt you, so you are through with family. You shouldn't do that! Jesus did not let His hurt emotions change God's plan for Him and us.

What did the apostles do after Jesus ascended? They replaced Judas. They took no wasted time grieving over their lost friend. They moved on to another leader. Matthias took Judas' place. This was all within seven days after Jesus' ascension.

That is what you have to do. You can't continue to grieve over lost friends. You must replace them. I am not suggesting that you get married right after your divorce, but, I am saying, "Move on with your life." Maybe you don't get married right away but you can go out with friends and do things that your former spouse would not do with you. If your ex did not like sports, but you did, go to a game. If your ex did not like camping, go camping. If your ex did not like dancing, take dancing lessons. Don't live in regret. Replace the bad soul ties with good ones.

JONATHAN AND DAVID

Contrast Judas with Jonathan, and you'll see a glaring difference. There are three characteristics of a good soul tie, and you see all three in the life of Jonathan:

1. GOOD SOUL TIES ARE BASED ON A LEGAL CONTRACT.

First Samuel 18:3 says, *"Jonathan made a covenant with David."* There is a loyalty based on covenant.

If you are married, don't be fooled by another person vying for your affection. Your marriage is the legal contract you are in, and you owe loyalty to your partner. The devil will tell you, "Your spouse is not God's choice for you. This other person is better. They understand you."

No! I don't care how affectionate and understanding the other person is—you are not in a covenant with them. You can never have a good, soul-tie-breaking covenant with your spouse. Period!

If you feel attraction toward someone else's spouse, don't act on it. I don't care how much you feel for this person, they are in a covenant with another. You should not tamper with that covenant.

It is interesting to note that Judas left the Last Supper to betray Christ. The Last Supper was the ratification of the covenant that Jesus made with us. Judas did not finish the covenant. This was a sign that he was a bad soul tie.

When a boyfriend tells his girl, "I love you. Please, let's have sex," she needs to sing the Beyoncé song, "If you liked it, you should have put a ring on it." The song makes a great point. Don't give your very best—even losing your virginity—to someone who wants your whole self, but does not want to make a covenant with you.

Too many people are giving themselves wholly and unconditionally to people who refuse to make a covenant with them. Don't be fooled into entering a soul tie based on emotion. Make sure there is a covenant behind your relationship.

DON'T BE FOOLED INTO ENTERING A SOUL TIE BASED ON EMOTION. MAKE SURE THERE IS A COVENANT BEHIND YOUR RELATIONSHIP.

This goes also for business, work, and ministry. Many will try to take advantage of you, expecting you to give yourself, your time, and your money, yet they don't want to make a covenant with you. This is a bad omen. Don't fall for it.

2. GOOD SOUL TIES ARE BASED ON UNSELFISH LOVE.

"Jonathan made a covenant with David because he loved him as himself" (1 Samuel 18:3). Jonathan loved David as himself. He followed the golden rule: do to others as you would have them do to you. A good soul tie will be based on selflessness. Sometimes, a person will be willing to make a covenant, but for selfish reasons. They want something from you; they are not looking to be a blessing to you.

Your friendships must be based on an absolute concern for each other. This means that you both must be willing to lay down your lives for each other. You can't bail and run at the first sign of trouble.

The prodigal son left his covenant relationship with his unselfish father, and joined in illicit relationships with selfish people. When the prodigal's money ran out, so did his friends.

A friend is willing to drive with you even when you lose your limousine.

My dad was a bar owner. He thought he had many friends. But when he suffered a stroke, none of his friends visited him in the hospital or even called to check up on him. One bartender did call to ask my dad for money. I rebuked her, "You did not even visit my dad in the hospital. Now he is at my house, and you did not even ask if you could visit him to see how he is doing. Instead, you called because you needed money. You should be ashamed of yourself." Needless to say, she never called back.

After a couple of years, his best friend called to see how he was doing. I told him, "I don't understand you and all the bar friends. You were one of my dad's best friends and his business partner, yet you have not even visited once." He felt guilty and rightly came to visit him.

There was, in contrast, a steady stream of visitors from my church to visit my dad. My dad, who was not saved at the time of his stroke, came to the Lord because he saw that his true friends were members of my church.

My dad broke down in tears and told a visiting minister, "None of my friends have visited me to see how I am doing. Only the church members have visited me." The guest minister led my dad in the sinner's prayer. I later baptized him.

Are you connected to a selfish person? Are you the one making nearly all the sacrifices to maintain the relationship? It's possible that you are in a bad relationship. If it is your spouse, then you will have put up with it and pray that your spouse becomes more giving; the same with your parents and children. For others, you are not so bound—get out of it if you can.

3. GOOD SOUL TIES ARE BASED ON PEOPLE FIGHTING FOR YOU, NOT AGAINST YOU.

"Jonathan took off the robe he was wearing and gave it to David, along with his tunic, and even his sword, his bow and his belt" (1 Samuel 18:4). Jonathan gave David his weapons. He was saying that he would fight for David. He would never be David's enemy.

Jonathan's commitment was tested when his father wanted David dead. Jonathan risked his life by saving David from his father's hand. It took courage for Jonathan to keep his word, but he did it.

This is the highest form of friendship. If you can find a friend who will be totally loyal to you and fight for you, then do not let them go! They are a rare jewel.

You might be in a relationship in which your so-called friend actually fights against you. They may work at destroying your self-esteem, your financial future, and your physical, emotional, and spiritual health. That is a bad soul tie. Break it!

Judas failed at all three points. He failed to enter a covenant with Jesus, he sold His friendship for thirty pieces of silver, and he brought soldiers to fight and capture Jesus.

Do the people you have soul ties with resemble Jonathan or Judas? Also, make sure that you are a Jonathan to others. You can't expect good friends if you fail to be a good friend. At every point in your life, you need friendships. Just make sure those relationships are benefiting you, rather than hurting you.

SIX

NOT GOOD TO BE ALONE

The Lord *God said, "It is not good for the man to be alone. I will make a helper suitable for him."* (Genesis 2:18)

God admitted that His relationship with Adam was not enough for Adam. Adam needed more than divine companionship; he needed human companionship. Sometimes, overly spiritual people will say, "I don't need anyone! I just need God!" It sounds good, but it's not true. Usually people speak that way out of hurt. As much as Adam loved and appreciated fellowship with God, he needed another creature like himself to feel complete.

Don't think it strange that you feel a similar need to be with others. As strong as your relationship with God is, you still need human relationships. It would be strange if you did not feel that need. Monks have given the need for soul ties a bad name. They give the impression that all they need is God, that it is somehow holier to live alone with only prayer and meditation. That is all good, but we humans need to sit down and eat with others. We need to pray with others. We need to talk with others. We need to work with others. And for those of us called to marriage, we need intimacy.

I hate when people describe their love for God in sexual terms. God is not a male or female. He is altogether different from you and me. You still need a spouse (at least most do). God can fulfill those needs that only the Creator could fulfill—namely, salvation. Yet even while He saved you, He put you in God's family. He built the church. The church has a steeple, but it also has people!

He intends for you to work out your salvation with fear and trembling and with other people. You are not to be a loner. There are too many loners in the body of Christ. This is not healthy. It is not God's plan for you to be a loner. Don't be afraid that others will hurt you. Let me remove any doubt: *people will hurt you.* It happens. But the alternative is worse. To avoid people because they will hurt you is a tragic mistake.

So God took responsibility to make a *"helper suitable"* for Adam. God is the mastermind of relationships. He thought of it. He makes others for you, just as He makes you for others.

MONKEY OR SPOUSE?

It is interesting that after God declared to Adam his need for human companionship, God brought him the animals to see what he would name them. *"Now the Lord God had formed out of the ground all the beasts of the field and all the birds of the air. He brought them to the man to see what he would name them; and whatever the man called each living creature, that was its name"* (Genesis 2:19).

There is a life lesson in this story. You have to be able to discern between a monkey and a friend. You have to know the difference between an ape and a wife. In life, God will bring you different people and you have to know their place in your life. If you give to someone a place of deep friendship when they should only be an acquaintance, then you will eventually get hurt. That acquaintance is not meant to be your close friend. If you give your close friends the role of a teacher, you may have trouble for yourself. Your friends are not always to be your prime mentor.

IF YOU GIVE YOUR CLOSE FRIENDS THE ROLE OF A TEACHER, YOU MAY HAVE TROUBLE FOR YOURSELF. YOUR FRIENDS ARE NOT ALWAYS TO BE YOUR PRIME MENTOR.

There is a passage from Ecclesiasticus 6:6 that gives wise advice: "Be in peace with many, nevertheless have but one counsellor of a thousand"[1] (KJV). Its author, Jesus, the son of Sirach of Jerusalem, admitted that we need thousands of friends and acquaintances, but we are not to make everyone our counselor. Know people's place in your life. Relationships are a blessing, provided you know the limitations and expectations of each one.

1. Ecclesiasticus was once part of the King James Version of the Bible, but was removed in 1885. So for two hundred and seventy-four years, it was part of the KJV Bible. Martin Luther said that the Apocrypha is not regarded as equal to the Holy Scriptures, yet was profitable and good to read.

Your spouse, for example, may be a wonderful helpmate, but not necessarily your teacher. In fact, Peter warns that if husbands need instruction, it won't necessarily come from their wives. He says to the wives: "[Husbands] *may be won over without words by the behavior of their wives, when they see the purity and reverence of your lives*" (1 Peter 3:1–2).

When a spouse, friend, or coworker demands that they become your counselor, you need to remind them of their place in your life. You have your pastor! He may not be your close friend, but he is your counselor. It is a mistake to make people close to you your spiritual advisers. Don't do that. You create an ungodly soul tie, not because the person does not belong in your life, but because you exalted them to a position that God did not call them to be in your life.

On the other hand, don't necessarily expect your pastor to be your best pal, because that usually does not happen. He can, however, still be your spiritual advisor.

So when God brings a giraffe to Adam, he is to know its place in the garden. If he needs fruit on some high branches, he knows who to call.

Every person has a place in your life. They will be a blessing to you when you give them the right "name." Wouldn't it be tragic if Adam looked at a monkey and called it "wife"? Ouch!

That's what you might have done in your life. God brought you people in your life, and you may have given them a wrong name. God brought you a friend, and you named them "business partner." God brought you a business partner, and you named them "friend." Pastor, God has brought many church members, but you called them "board members." Not everyone is called to those places. What could have been a good soul tie has turned tragic because you have given people the wrong name and place in your life.

SOMEONE WHO IS A HELPER

"I will make a helper...for him." God brings people to you who will help you in your life. He does not bring people to make you work harder to maintain the relationships. All relationships should be helpful to all involved. No one should be burdened with working incredibly hard to keep the relationships in good working order. That is a burdensome relationship, not a helpful one.

NO ONE SHOULD BE BURDENED WITH WORKING INCREDIBLY HARD TO KEEP THE RELATIONSHIPS IN GOOD WORKING ORDER. THAT IS A BURDENSOME RELATIONSHIP, NOT A HELPFUL ONE.

I agree to a certain extent that relationships take work, but not to such a degree that you are better off without the relationship. You should not have to walk on "pins and needles" with people.

Adam needed help. Eve was that help.

My wife, Sonia, and I have been married for well over thirty years, and the relationship for both of us is a blessing. It's a blessing because I can work less and still get more done because she is at my side. The same is true for Sonia. I am able to provide things in our marriage that she could not provide for herself. That's a healthy relationship.

If you find yourself working harder to be with someone than not to be with them, something is terribly wrong! If you spend a lot of time arguing and losing joy over the relationship, then things must change! Relationships must be a blessing to all involved.

There was a couple that joined our church, and it soon became clear, from my perspective, that the woman had made a terrible mistake by marrying this man. He had gotten out of prison and told the woman that he would start to go to church to make her happy, so she consented to marry him.

The relationship, however, was completely one-sided. She made all the money. She got up early in the morning to make breakfast and take her daughter to school on her way to work. It was her biological child, not his. The husband, out of necessity, picked up the daughter from school, but never lifted a finger to clean the house or make dinner for the family. After the wife came home from work, she then cooked dinner and cleaned the entire house, before getting the child washed and ready for bed. By the time she got into bed, she was exhausted. On top of this, her husband was an incredibly jealous and angry man who regularly cursed and complained about his wife, and didn't even try to get a job.

Eventually, while she accepted his laziness, she would not put up with his verbal and, on rare occasions, physical abuse. She left him and left town. She told me that she was scared of him, and knew the only way to be free from him was to leave the city of El Paso.

The husband, without any money or place to go, pleaded with me to talk to his wife about taking him back. I told him, "Look, there is only one way she will want to come back, and that is if it is worth it for her. She obviously loved you. She would not have married you if she didn't. But you have to make yourself attractive and a great catch by improving your own life. You must first get a good job. That is your first step."

The man got angry with me for suggesting that he needed to work. He wanted his wife to come back to the same situation. It wasn't going to happen! You see, the wife recognized the bad soul tie she had with her husband. She saw it! No one wants to stay in a relationship where the other person is not a helper. You don't want it, and neither does anyone want it from you.

SOMEONE WHO IS SUITABLE

The other part of God making a helper was creating one that was "suitable" for Adam. *Suitable* means fitting. I wear a size forty-two in suits. I will try on a suit, and if it doesn't fit, I don't wear it. It doesn't mean the suit is worthless; it just means it is not fitting for me.

Have you ever passed by a shoe store and saw a pair of shoes you wanted so badly? You go in the store and tell the salesperson, "I want to try on those shoes. My size is a seven." The salesperson goes in the back and says they only have size six. Despite the fact that you know that it is the wrong size, you try it on. It hurts, but it looks good on you. Reluctantly, you buy the shoes, only to find that they hurt your feet. Eventually, you regret buying the shoes. They just were not fitting for you!

This is the same with relationships. You want so badly to have this person in your life. They look good. They smell good. But the fit is all wrong. Regardless, you start the romance anyway. Mistake!

I am convinced that my wife is a perfect fit for me. People have said, "Sonia is such a follower. She absolutely adores her husband and will submit to him." Others lie and say she worships me. She doesn't. I am a very strong leader, and I did not need to marry a leader type. If I did, we would have butt heads all the time. I thank God that my wife has the temperament to be my spouse. Not many women could have put up with me.

GOD PUTS YOU TOGETHER WITH OTHERS THAT WILL FIT YOU. NOT EVERYONE FITS YOU. IT DOESN'T MEAN THAT THEY WILL NOT FIT ANOTHER PERSON, BUT THEY DON'T FIT YOU.

God puts you together with others that will fit you. Not everyone fits you. It doesn't mean that they will not fit another person, but they don't fit you. You need to understand where people should fit in your life.

DIFFERENT FITS FOR DIFFERENT PEOPLE

The reason we need many churches is because there are many personality types. One church does not fit all! My church fits a lot of people, but I don't pretend that my church is a perfect fit for everyone. I think it is a fit for most!

Similarly, God has a perfect job for you. It will fit you. The mistake is to take jobs that do not fit you.

Let me give you an example. When I was single and young, the church I attended knew I needed a job, so they pulled some strings and got me an interview with a rich member who owned a lot of property. At the interview, the ladies said they needed a "handyman" for the office. If you know me, you are falling on the floor laughing. I am a lot of things, but a handyman is not one of them.

To prove my point, one time the light in our downstairs restroom went out, and my wife asked me to fix it. Instead of humbling myself by asking for help, I unscrewed the cover of the light switch. I looked at it and thought, *Maybe it just needs some WD-40.* I sprayed it and then flicked the switch. Sparks flew all over the place, and the rest of the lights went out! After that, the light in our bedroom would go on and off without anyone touching the switch. It was like a ghost lived in our house. Like I said, I am not a handyman.

Knowing that about myself, I looked at the ladies at the real-estate company and told them, "I really appreciate the job offer, but I will be a disappointment for you. I do not know anything about handy work." They tried to convince me that it was a simple job, but I rightly declined the offer. Later, I got a job at a restaurant. I still enjoy cooking. This is where I flourished.

People are like suits. Not every person fits you perfectly. Make sure you cultivate the relationships that are suitable for you. Even if it is too late to make changes, you can still tailor the relationships, like you can tailor suits. It takes great wisdom to do so, but it can be done. Christ lives in you and He will give you the wisdom to tailor the relationships in your life. You can make your marriage work. You can make the relationships work with your parents and children. Learn to tailor the relationships in your life until they are "fitting" for everyone.

SEVEN

GOD CREATES THE NEED FOR GOOD SOUL TIES

It was God who expressed the need for Adam to have a wife, not Adam. God said, *"It is not good for the man to be alone"* (Genesis 2:18). Adam was not walking alone in the garden, kicking the rocks, feeling sorry for himself that he was alone. He was not moaning and complaining, saying, "God, I am so lonely. All the animals have partners, but not me. It's not fair. I need someone badly!"

Adam did not feel the need to enter a relationship. He felt complete in himself. He was truly single—separate, complete, unique, and whole. Single should simply mean that you are not fractured. Adam's soul was whole. He was not a fragmented man who craved intimacy with a woman.

Even after God mentioned that it was not good for the man to be alone, God allowed him to be alone for a little while longer. I think the lesson is that you need to learn to be alone and take care of yourself before you can be ready for an intimate relationship.

Sex makes you "one" with another person. Too many broken people try achieve wholeness through sex, but only attaches your brokenness to another person. Sex outside of marriage will not make you whole because another person cannot make you whole!

Myles Munroe used to say that a two-egg omelet is only good if both eggs are good. If one egg is rotten, it ruins the other egg. If one person is broken and not whole going into a relationship, then the relationship will be rotten. This is the root of bad soul ties. If one or both are sick in their souls, then they will inevitably create an unhealthy soul tie.

CONTENTMENT AS A SINGLE PERSON

God wanted Adam to experience time alone with Him so that he could be whole, not fractured or broken! Adam fellowshipped with God and enjoyed sweet communion with Him. He was content!

Like Adam, you need to be content with your life. Paul wrote, *"Seek not a wife"* (1 Corinthians 7:27 KJV). He did not say that you should not get married, only that you should not spend your days desperately seeking and searching for marriage. Be content as a single person. Learn to enjoy your relationship with God and with others before you enter into the most important relationship of your life with a spouse.

Don't make the mistake of going from one relationship to another, hoping you will find that special someone who makes you feel whole. Take time off. Paul even encouraged married couples to take a sabbatical from their intimate relationship, *"Do not deprive each other except by mutual consent and for a time, so that you may devote yourselves to prayer. Then come together again so that Satan will not tempt you because of your lack of self-control"* (1 Corinthians 7:5). The purpose of that time of separation is to get close to the Lord. You need to keep your intimacy with God strong in order for your relationship with your spouse to become stronger.

IF YOU ARE AFRAID OF COMMITMENT, THIS MAY STEM FROM BAD EXPERIENCES, EITHER FROM HOME OR ELSEWHERE. IT MAY BE NECESSARY FOR YOU TO EXPLORE THIS THROUGH COUNSELING BEFORE YOU WILL BE READY TO CONFIDENTLY MOVE FORWARD IN A RELATIONSHIP WITHOUT THE CONSTANT FEAR OF BEING HURT.

While Jesus was a people person—He loved company—He also took time to be alone with God: *"He withdrew by boat privately to a solitary place"* (Matthew 14:13). You have to enjoy being alone. You can't always hang out around people. Take a break from your cell phone and from social media. There are times you must get to a solitary place to pray and read the Word. Listen to sermons. This helps you in your relationships with others, especially with your spouse.

This is what God did with Adam. He made Adam wait for his spouse. Be patient, like Adam. Wait for the right person; don't be quick to jump into bed with anyone; take your time! Adam was so totally unique and whole that he did not miss others when he was alone. He was so "together," so separate and so complete in himself that he did not even know he needed anyone else.

This is not to say that you should be intentionally avoiding marriage like the plague. This opposite extreme forgets that marriage is good and a blessing. If you are afraid of commitment, this may stem from bad experiences, either from home or elsewhere. It may be necessary for you to explore this through counseling before you will be ready to confidently move forward in a relationship without the constant fear of being hurt. Godly soul ties are created between people who are whole, not people who are broken.

THE MISSING RIB

What made Adam finally want to get married? God put into his heart the desire to be attached to Eve, after God took something out of him.

> *So the* L*ORD God caused the man to fall into a deep sleep; and while he was sleeping, he took one of the man's ribs and closed up the place with flesh. Then the* L*ORD God made a woman from the rib he had taken out of the man, and he brought her to the man. The man said, "This is now bone of my bones and flesh of my flesh; she shall be called 'woman,' for she was taken out of man."* (Genesis 2:21–23)

Adam was completely whole, missing nothing, until God took a rib from him. Adam was now missing a rib. By joining to Eve, Adam found his rib, his missing part.

This does not mean you should be walking around looking for your rib, or a man with a missing rib. No! The idea is that Adam was complete and whole, until God took the rib. When Adam sensed a lack, he knew he needed a partner.

There will come a time in your life after you have walked in wholeness when you will meet someone whom you feel you can't live without. There is something special about that person. When that happens, it will be because God took the rib from you, or in other words, you feel a lack that can only be filled by this person. It hits you: this is what you've been looking for.

Too many people are missing things other than their rib. They miss their brains! They don't use common sense to navigate the relationships of life. Others are missing their hearts. Their hearts have been taken out and trampled on by others so that they become easily moved with emotions and become attracted to bad relationships. Is this you?

God did not take from Adam his brain or his heart, but his rib. You can live without a rib. It is the same with marriage. You can live without getting married—you won't die. If you find yourself feeling as though you desperately need someone else, then you need God to heal your mind and heart before you need Him to take out a rib.

A rib is a bone that is near the heart. God will open your eyes at the right time to show you your missing rib. But first, you must walk in wholeness. Do not think you are missing a rib yet! You still have your rib. Bad theology teaches that everyone is missing someone in their lives and that they will not be complete until they find that missing person. That is a romantic notion. It creates what I call the "Romeo and Juliet syndrome." I call it this because no one human is so important that you should commit suicide over them if you can't be with them. That's crazy!

The moral lesson we can learn from Adam was that he only felt the need to be with Eve when he woke up from his sleep. This showed that Adam was not creating the relationship. He was not trying to make it happen. How could he have had anything to do with making the wife if he was asleep? The lesson is that Adam did not try to create something to fulfill his need, God did! Adam did not spend his whole life with a missing rib. He was complete throughout his life until God created a need within him. When that happens, *then* you are ready for marriage.

Listen to these wise words from one of the most romantic poets of all time: *"Do not arouse or awaken love until it so desires"* (Song of Songs 2:7; 8:4). There is a time when romantic love will grip you, but don't let lust or brokenness awaken that romantic love. Let God *"awaken"* you from your sleep, and you will find yourself ready to get married. You will be ready to tie the knot, and you will create a godly soul tie with your spouse!

PART III
THE BROKEN SOUL

EIGHT

STOCKHOLM SYNDROME

In 1973, police surrounded a bank in Norrmalmstorg square in Stockholm, Sweden. A bank robber was holding four customers hostage inside the bank vault. By the second day, the hostages were on a first-name basis with their captor. When the hostages had an opportunity to escape, they did not. They were only freed on the fifth day when the police drove them out by pumping tear gas into the vault. Even then, the hostages held on to their captor, shielding him from being shot by the police. Later, the former hostages even raised money for his criminal defense.

This case puzzled investigators. Why would people who were threatened by another human being develop a strange attraction to that person? Psychologists eventually termed this strange attraction *Stockholm syndrome*. They recognized that victims of harassment, threats, abuse, or intimidation can develop a strong emotional tie to the person hurting them.

As a pastor, I have seen examples of such behavior play out in the real lives of ordinary people.

GETTING FREE

Pastor Jerry kept a secret from everyone except his wife. He had a strange attraction to men. He knew it was wrong, but it was there, haunting him. He could not tell anyone because in his church, homosexuality was considered to be the most taboo of all sins, except for pedophilia.

While he was a good man, a good pastor, and even had a flourishing church, this same-sex attraction made him feel miserable. He felt he was unworthy of the position of a minister. He could not confide in anyone about this weakness because he feared the secret would leak out and ruin his marriage and church. He also knew that he needed to confess to someone. He believed in practicing the passage in James 5:16, "*Therefore confess your sins to each other and pray for each other so that you may be healed.*" He saw people healed as they confessed their sins to him; now he needed healing, also. He knew God had forgiven him, but he wanted to be healed of this sin. He believed that by confessing to an elder and having the elder pray for him, he would be healed.

That is when he contacted me. He traveled a great distance to see me. When we met, he fidgeted a little. Finally, after some chitchat, he said, "This is very hard for me to do. I have kept a secret from everyone except my wife. I have homosexual feelings, and I can't stand them. I need to be healed." He broke down and wept.

After he got his composure, I asked him, "Brother, when was the last time you acted on these feelings?"

"Before I was married, I had encounters with different men. Actually, I had sexual encounters with women as well. I have not cheated on my wife since we have been married, except for watching pornography. But every time I look at it, I feel dirty, and I always ask God to forgive me."

I asked, "So are you attracted to both male and female?"

"Yes, I always have been since I can remember. I like them both, but being attracted to men is sickening to me. I don't want this attraction."

I then asked Pastor Jerry, "Were you ever sexually raped or abused when you were young by an older man?"

He looked shocked. "Yes! When I was six, an older man sexually molested me. I was so scared and ashamed. I felt I could not tell my father because I feared he would beat me. Then, when I was about twelve, my uncle raped me."

I explained Stockholm syndrome to Jerry. "Brother Jerry, you were a victim when you were a child. These older men committed a crime against you! If this had not happened, you would not have these homosexual feelings. The abuse has so wounded you that it has affected your psyche. Whether you realize it or not, when people wound you, it can develop a strange attraction to the type of people who hurt you. That is what has happened in your case."

This helped brother Jerry to let go of any guilt; he was first a victim before he sinned. It helped him to realize that he did not choose homosexual attraction; it was something that chose him. Then I led Jerry into a prayer for inner healing. Later in this book, I will lead you in the same prayer that I prayed with Jerry.

Two days later, Jerry emailed me to tell me how free he was! I believe you will be free, too.

FATAL ATTRACTION

Why do you keep doing the things you do that you don't want to do? Why do you find yourself attracted to all the wrong people?

The nice guy at church does not attract you, but the bad boy at the club turns your motor on. The sweet Christian at the prayer meeting, while you love her in Christ, holds no attraction for you, but the floozy at work—now *she* is attractive!

"There are not any good single men at church!" That is the mantra of many single women. The truth is that there are plenty of single men at church, but the women don't find them attractive. Why? Is it possible that they are looking for love and attraction in the people who have either hurt them or neglected them?

The book and movie *Fifty Shades of Grey* illustrates attraction to abusers. In the story, Ana meets a rich businessman named Christian. He is the opposite of being a Christian. He is into sexual bondage and convinces Ana to go along with his fetishes. Ana even signs a contract with Christian, which reads: "The Submissive shall accept whippings, floggings, spankings, caning, paddlings, or any other discipline the Dominant should decide to administer, without hesitation, inquiry, or complaint."[2] Ana is not the first to sign this contract. She is the sixteenth woman to do so.

The movie was a flop, thank God, but the books were bestsellers.

---

2. E. L. James, *Fifty Shades of Grey* (New York: Vintage Books, 2012), 170.

Researchers at the University of Michigan conducted a study on the relationship between "health risks and reading popular fiction depicting violence against women."[3] The research showed that women who read the *Fifty Shades* trilogy were 25 percent more likely to have an abusive partner, 34 percent more likely to have a partner who stalked them, and 65 percent more likely to engage in binge drinking. The books pervert the meaning of love.

My stomach sinks when I think of the women who found this story compelling and who found Christian to be attractive. What is it about them that made the book series a runaway success? Is it the fact that they feel unworthy of a good guy, or, even worse, that they are attracted to bad men?

Kelly comes to my mind. She is a nice person, people like her, and she is also very pretty. Yet when she was in school, Kelly never liked the nice boys. Instead, she liked the bad boys—the older the better. Eventually, she married three times, always to men who were much older than her and who were alcoholics.

After talking to Kelly about her bad choices, she told me that her father was an alcoholic. He was never there for her. She hated him. I pointed out her strange attraction to older men who were alcoholics. Then I asked, "Don't you see the connection with your father and these three former husbands?"

She answered, "I did think about how these men seemed to be so much like my father."

"By being neglected by your father," I explained, "you have had a desire to be loved by your father, so you have picked men who were just like him, in the false belief that their love

---

3. "Reading 'Fifty Shades' Linked to Unhealthy Behaviors," *MSU TODAY*, August 21, 2014, http://msutoday.msu.edu/news/2014/reading-fifty-shades-linked-to-unhealthy-behaviors/ (accessed July 12, 2017).

could somehow replace the love you did not have from your father."

Her eyes teared up! I led her into the prayer for inner healing. She too, like Jerry, was set free from her terrible, destructive attraction.

WOUNDS CREATE ATTRACTION

As I said in chapter 7, Adam had no desire to be married until God took a rib from his side. At the moment, when he woke from his deep sleep, he wanted Eve! The desire came after God took something away from Adam—his rib. The wound in Adam's side created a new desire. Adam desired the very thing that he lost! Eve was his lost rib. He was attracted to his rib. Do you see how desire is created? It is created by loss that awakens the realization of a need.

The devil works differently than God. He also works by creating loss. Unlike God, however, who does it painlessly, the devil does not put you into a deep sleep. Nor does he take a simple bone like a rib—one that you could live without. Instead, he creates pain by maliciously wounding you. He does not put you under anesthesia to keep from hurting you; instead, you are wide awake, with all your nerves, senses, and feelings—aware of the pain—while he breaks you. He wounds you through neglect, abuse, rape, or even something as simple as the verbal barrage of hate. These wounds are hurtful, and, unfortunately, they create an attraction for the very same people, or type of people, who have hurt you.

This explains why you are attracted to abusers. This explains why you develop soul ties with the wrong people.

NINE

TAKING RESPONSIBILITY WITHOUT EXCUSE

The plane was thirty-three thousand feet in the air and was headed back to the US. After being refreshed by a short nap, I opened my Kindle Bible and began to read a famous passage from Psalm 51. Suddenly, these verses opened their meaning to me. Never before had I seen this Scripture in this way. It is David's repentance after falling into sin with Bathsheba and eventually putting her husband in harm's way in the battle, where he was killed.

> *Surely I was sinful at birth, sinful from the time my mother conceived me. Yet you desired faithfulness even in the womb;*

you taught me wisdom in that secret place.
(Psalm 51:5–6 NIV11)

NO EXCUSES

Maybe you can relate to David. He was *"sinful at birth."* This is not to say that he was speaking of original sin—although I believe in it. Rather, he was making a statement about his own life. You see, David did not begin life in the right way. Another way to say it is that he was "born in sin." David was an illegitimate child. This is explains why he looked different than his brothers, and why his father, Jesse, was embarrassed to bring David as one of his own children to be examined by the prophet, Samuel, who was searching for the son who was to be anointed. After all, the prophet said that God told him to anoint one of Jesse's sons as the next king. Jesse thought that being an illegitimate son disqualified David from the office.

As Jesse reluctantly fetched David, the Bible says about David's appearance, *"He was ruddy, with a fine appearance and handsome features"* (1 Samuel 16:12). There would be no reason to mention his physical features if he looked the same as his brothers. The word *"ruddy"* comes from the Hebrew word *admoniy*, which means "reddish (of the hair or the complexion)." It possibly referred to red hair or a light complexion. Either way, he looked dissimilar from his brothers. His appearance seems to be a mark that he was not from his brothers' mother. He had a different mother. Who was she?

All David said about his mother was that *"in sin did my mother conceive me"* (Psalm 51:5 KJV). He acknowledged that his life began in sin, that he did not have the right childhood. He was rejected by his father and brothers. Later, when David becomes the son-in-law of the king, he was rejected by him also. David knew rejection!

In Psalm 51, David contemplates his life. How could he have committed adultery and plotted the murder of Bathsheba's husband? Why did he do such a wicked thing before God? As he meditates on his sin, he realizes one thing about his life: he grew up with rejection. He was messed up! Someone as messed up as David can understand his sin a little better. Someone broken can easily break! He broke—he gave in to temptation.

Maybe you can relate to David's life. Maybe you have a similar profession: "Like David, I am so broken. I had a terrible childhood. I was rejected by my mother and father. I was abused by those I trusted. My life has been a total wreck! I now understand why I do the terrible things I do. I understand why I am attracted to the wrong people; why I keep getting involved in destructive soul ties."

Psychologists have done a fine job of explaining how we react to our environment, yet they are lousy at explaining the solution. They often pat the patient on the head, saying, "I understand you. Do you not realize that you do what you do because of your parents? They are at fault. It's not your fault, but theirs."

But that is where David departs from modern psychologists. While acknowledging his terrible past, he does not blame his father or mother for his sin. David exclaims: "*Yet you desired faithfulness even in the womb; you taught me wisdom in that secret place*" (Psalm 51:6 NIV11).

David was saying that despite his bad upbringing, despite his parental rejection, God demanded him to be faithful! Not just faithful in life, but faithful "*even in the womb.*" How could he be faithful in the womb? He was simply saying that he had no excuse for what he had done against God. He could not blame his mother, although he understood her sin. He could not blame his father, although he understood why he treated him so badly. David was saying that although God understood where the sin in David came from, God would not allow him to make excuses for his sin!

Like David, you might understand why you are attracted to sinful behavior, but it is no excuse. It might be a reason, but it is never an excuse!

You will never be able to break ungodly soul ties by making excuses for your sin. While it is good and therapeutic to understand why you do the wrong things, understanding is not an excuse to continue to do the wrong things. You must take responsibility for your life; otherwise, you will not change!

WHILE IT IS GOOD AND THERAPEUTIC TO UNDERSTAND WHY YOU DO THE WRONG THINGS, UNDERSTANDING IS NOT AN EXCUSE TO CONTINUE TO DO THE WRONG THINGS. YOU MUST TAKE RESPONSIBILITY FOR YOUR LIFE; OTHERWISE, YOU WILL NOT CHANGE!

I am aware that many priests were sexually abused in their youth by older priests. I read a story about one young boy in my city who was sexual abused by two priests in El Paso. Despite the pain he went through, he still wanted to be a priest. This scares me! It's good to desire to be a minister, but I fear that, without healing, the brokenness of this young man will likely lead to him abusing other young boys. If he does, there is no excuse for his sinful behavior. Of course, in compassion, we can understand how broken he is, but there is no excuse for his behavior if he operates out of that brokenness.

It helped David to know where his sin sprung from. Like his father and mother, whose sin resulted in his birth, he saw that he had acted out the actions of his parents. Just as they had sinned sexually, David had done the same thing! Yet, David knew that if he was ever going to overcome this sexual weakness, he had to recognize where the sin came from, and, more importantly, he had to take responsibility for his sin!

The same is true for you. In the previous chapter, I explained how pain can create soul ties. If the pain is created by the devil, he will use it to create ungodly soul ties. It is good to be aware of your soul—your psyche. But you still must take responsibility for your life. You can't blame your parents, the molester, or your ex-spouse for the actions of your life. You must declare, "The sin stops here! God demands faithfulness of me, even in the womb. If He demands me to be faithful in the womb, then surely He demands me to be faithful as an adult. I will be faithful to God."

THE COVER-UP IS WORSE THAN THE CRIME

> *Have mercy on me, O God, according to your unfailing love; according to your great compassion blot out my transgressions. Wash away all my iniquity and cleanse me from my sin.* (Psalm 51:1–2)

The first thing you must do is ask for mercy! Forget about trying to understand your own soul, first understand that you need mercy from God. You might say, "But I keep doing the same stupid things over again. I think God is tired of me coming back with the same sin to confess."

I understand. But let me say this: you will get tired of your sin—hopefully sooner than later—before God ever grows tired of forgiving you for your sin. I know sometimes you can feel like a hypocrite for doing the same things, over and over again, but it is important to know that for every sin you commit, you can still confess them to God. Do not get tired of confessing your sins to God. He is never tired of forgiving you.

The danger is when you begin to justify your sin. After sinning for so long, the devil can convince you to believe that you are not really sinning. That's when corruption sets into your life. The moment you give up trying to change is when you become corrupt. Sin is one thing; corruption is something else. Corruption is a continued lifestyle with the belief that the lifestyle is not immoral.

THE MOMENT YOU GIVE UP TRYING TO CHANGE IS WHEN YOU BECOME CORRUPT. SIN IS ONE THING; CORRUPTION IS SOMETHING ELSE. CORRUPTION IS A CONTINUED LIFESTYLE WITH THE BELIEF THAT THE LIFESTYLE IS NOT IMMORAL.

This is the true danger of the homosexual agenda. Homosexual activists try to legitimize sinful behavior. It is the legitimizing of the behavior that is more dangerous than the sin itself. God can forgive anyone, including someone committing homosexual acts. Heaven's mercy is not bankrupt when God forgives homosexuals. They can be forgiven as easily as someone who has a bad temper. Sin is sin! Sure, some sins are graver and can bring more pain than other sins, but God forgives all sins.

David's sin was very great. He had sex with a married woman and impregnated her. Then, in order to cover his sin, he brought her husband, Uriah, back from the battlefield and got him drunk to tempt him to have sex with his wife, so that he would think he was the father. When this ruse failed, David ordered Uriah to the front battle lines, and then instructed the officer in charge to withdraw the troops, leaving Uriah defenseless. Uriah was killed in battle, and David promptly married Bathsheba.

Now, c'mon! That is bad! Bad to the core! Don't tell me that homosexual action is worse than what David did. Yet, God forgave David, just as He will forgive you, no matter what you have done.

The important thing is that David admitted his sin. It's not so easy to admit you have done wrong, but admission is necessary to receive God's mercy.

In another Psalm, David said, "*Then I acknowledged my sin to you and did not cover up my iniquity. I said, 'I will confess my transgressions to the* Lord*'—and you forgave the guilt of my sin*" (Psalm 32:5). The opposite of confessing your sin is to "*cover up*" your iniquity. There are all sorts of ways you can cover up your sin: you can hide your sin, you can deny your sin, or you can justify your sin. Don't do it! Be honest with God. Stop hiding your sin, denying your sin, and justifying your sin. Confess it instead!

Don't say, "What's wrong with what I am doing? What I am doing is legal. Others do this all the time. There is nothing wrong with my behavior." No! Admit your sin—don't cover it up.

GET RID OF GUILT

Notice that David said, "*You forgave the guilt of my sin.*" Guilt is damaging; it cannot cleanse you or heal you even if it feels "right" to wallow in guilt. Satan will accuse you of your past sins and your present struggles. He will try to make you feel like a hypocrite. This will not lead you to a holy life.

You must accept the forgiveness from God. The moment God forgives your sin, stop feeling guilty over it. Guilt is a feeling of condemnation and fear. Get rid of the negative feelings you have about your sin. Also, stop fearing that the worst is going to happen to you because of your mistakes. Trust that God will bring you favor and blessings! Negative feelings just feed the mistaken idea that you deserve bad things to happen to you, which builds and builds until your soul actually becomes attracted to the bad things. Stop it! Start believing that God has forgiven you. Be positive that good is coming your way.

GOD DOES NOT WANT YOU TO CONTINUE WITH A GUILTY CONSCIENCE AFTER HE HAS FORGIVEN YOU. THE BLOOD OF CHRIST WASHES YOU FROM YOUR SIN.

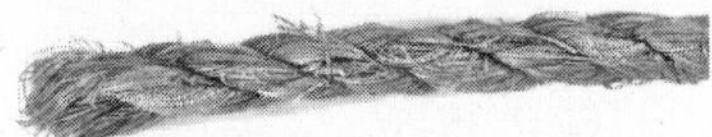

The Bible says this about the power of the blood of Christ: "*having our hearts sprinkled to cleanse us from a guilty conscience*" (Hebrews 10:22). A good conscience obviously helps lead you to do what is right. Someone with a bad conscience is one "*whose consciences have been seared as with a hot iron*" (1 Timothy 4:2). They feel no remorse or guilt over the evil deeds they do. A good conscience, however, is not the same as a guilty conscience. A good conscience will help you avoid wrong; but, when you have done wrong, then God wants you to be free from guilt. God does not want you to continue with a guilty conscience after He has forgiven you. The blood of Christ washes you from your sin.

If David had continued in guilt over his sin, it would have robbed him of the wisdom and courage to be leader. No leader can guide the people when they are racked with guilt. Guilt robs you of faith. It makes you feel like your prayers are unworthy of being answered. It steals from you the gifts that God has given you. You will feel too intimidated to use your gifts. Guilt will make you loathe yourself! You will act like a worm; you will crawl into the dirt; you won't live clean for long. The guilt will drive you into darker, dirtier places!

CLEANSE ME FROM MY SIN

David did not see God merely forgiving him, because he knew that God would do more: "*Wash away all my iniquity and cleanse me from my sin*" (Psalm 51:2). Sin makes you dirty. David did not want to continue living a dirty life, so he pleaded with God, "*Wash away all my iniquity.*"

Dirty people become attracted to dirty people. This is why you keep getting attracted to dirty people—you feel dirty. David desired cleansing. He wanted to come out of his sin clean and new again. The blood of Christ washes you like a detergent until you come out smelling clean. You notice that when you are clean, it's harder to allow yourself to get dirty again. After all, your clothes are so clean, so you try hard to keep them clean. Once your clothes get dirty, however, it becomes less important to keep more dirt from staining your clothes.

God wants you to know that He washes you from sin. He does not simply forgive you. Don't see yourself as a forgiven sinner. See yourself as a forgiven, cleansed saint. Saintly people get attracted to saintly people. See yourself as a saint!

WHO CARES WHAT OTHERS THINK?

David continued in this great psalm of repentance: *"For I acknowledge my transgressions: and my sin is ever before me"* (Psalm 51:3 KJV). David also admitted that people would view him differently because of his sin.

God's forgiveness and cleansing is for you personally. It doesn't affect the viewpoints of others. You cannot let people's view of you affect God's image of you. God is more merciful than any other person. No one will treat you with the kind of mercy that God shows you.

Sin removes God's guilt and condemnation, but it does not remove other people's condemnation of you. Allow people to have their own view of you, but do not let it affect your confidence before God. In order to underscore this point, David said, *"Against you, you only, have I sinned and done what is evil in your sight, so that you are proved right when you speak and justified when you judge"* (Psalm 51:4).

At first you might think that David forgot that he killed Uriah. But that's not what is going on here. Of course David knew Uriah was his victim! The point that David is bringing forth is simple: in the end, God's view of you is the only one that counts! David sinned against Uriah, and by so doing, actually sinned against God Himself. He understood the seriousness of his sin!

On Judgment Day, you will not stand before your father or mother, your pastor or priest, or any of your victims. You will stand before God alone! Why do you care what others think of you?

The apostle Paul understood this well:

> *I care very little if I am judged by you or by any human court; indeed, I do not even judge myself. My conscience is clear, but that does not make me innocent. It is the Lord who judges me.* (1 Corinthians 4:3–4)

Ungodly soul ties are strengthened when you fear others. You will be afraid to break soul ties when you fear people. You must not fear humans. Breaking free from fear brings strength to break any relationship that robs you of, or distorts, God's image of you. If you no longer fear people, you will no longer let them treat you like trash. As I told you before, do still love and pray for them, but do not be concerned with their view of you.

PART IV
HEALING FOR YOUR SOUL

TEN

CONFESS TO OTHERS

Sin is a disease. If it was just a decision, none of us would do it. The Bible teaches that Adam's sin resulted in us being made sinners. We are sinners by nature, not merely by choice. That is why we are so prone to form ungodly soul ties.

David described the nature of sin: *"For mine iniquities are gone over mine head: as an heavy burden they are too heavy for me"* (Psalm 38:4 KJV). This describes the power of sin; it's overwhelming; it's a weight beyond your ability to lift. You want to overcome it, but it is too much for you on your own.

However, once you come to Christ, you become born again and receive a new nature from God. That new nature is a nature of righteousness. You now have the ability, through the new birth, to live in a new way. As Paul wrote:

> *What shall we say, then? Shall we go on sinning so that grace may increase? By no means! We are those who have died to sin; how can we live in it any longer? Or don't you know that all of us who were baptized into Christ Jesus were baptized into his death? We were therefore buried with him through baptism into death in order that, just as Christ was raised from the dead through the glory of the Father, we too may live a new life.* (Romans 6:1–4 NIV11)

The passage is clear: because you are identified with Christ in His death and resurrection, you can "*live a new life.*" The challenge is that you still live in a body that is accustomed to living in a certain way. You might call them habits. The body still has bad habits from the previous life you lived, but now you have a new human spirit, born anew, so you have a new spiritual nature. One of the two—spirit or flesh—will win over the other in your life.

Even though you are born again—assuming you have accepted Christ and have been baptized—sin can be so embedded in your life that you need healing from it still. Peter writes to Christians, saying, "'*He himself bore our sins' in his body on the cross, so that we might die to sins and live for righteousness; 'by his wounds you have been healed.' For 'you were like sheep going astray,' but now you have returned to the Shepherd and Overseer of your souls*" (1 Peter 2:24–25 NIV11).

JESUS DIED TO HEAL YOU COMPLETELY—SPIRIT, SOUL, AND BODY. DON'T LIMIT THE HEALING POWER OF THE CROSS.

Jesus died to heal you completely—spirit, soul, and body. Don't limit the healing power of the cross. Just as your body might need further healing, so your soul might need further healing as well. When your soul has been broken—crushed and sick—you need Christ to heal you. You might have gone through devastating pain in life and as a result, have become *"like sheep going astray."* Yet you don't want to go astray. You want to return to the Shepherd and Overseer of your soul. How can you do this? Through the help and servant-guidance of leaders in the church. God has appointed shepherds of the church to help you return to God. God orders the elders to *"be shepherds of God's flock that is under your care, serving as overseers"* (1 Peter 5:2).

THE ROLE OF ELDERS

One of the great duties, callings, and anointing of the under-shepherds is the ability to bring healing to the soul. This is why Paul tells you and the elders, *"Brothers, if someone is caught in a sin, you who are spiritual should restore him gently"* (Galatians 6:1). The person who can help you is called the *"spiritual"* one. Not the perfect one, but simply someone who follows the leading of the Spirit. This spiritual one is usually a mature person in the Lord. The word *elder* means an older and more mature person. This is the person God uses to restore you.

The elder must always act *"gently,"* not harshly. The elder must be a forgiving person, not a resentful person, and the elder must believe that every soul can be restored. The elder must know that there is no sin greater than God's grace. The elder must not be too corrective. He or she must not discipline too harshly so as to not cause the sinner to feel too grieved. The elder must be a safe harbor for the repentant believer to confess their sins. The repentant believer must not be exposed to ridicule. The elder must keep the confession to himself, unless others could be harmed by the secrecy.

The ultimate goal of the elder is to *"restore"* the repentant believer. *Restore* means to mend what has been broken, to repair—not restored just to their condition before Christ, but rather to the condition Christ provided for them, a condition of total wholeness.

CONFESSING TO ELDERS

The elder cannot help you unless you are honest with him or her. This is why James commands:

> *Is anyone among you sick? Let them call the elders of the church to pray over him and anoint them with oil in the name of the Lord. And the prayer offered in faith will make the sick person well; the Lord will raise them up. If they have sinned, they will be forgiven. Therefore confess your sins to each other and pray for each other so that you may be healed. The prayer of a righteous person is powerful and effective.* (James 5:14–16 NIV11)

The sickness could be physical, but sometimes, it is spiritual. This is why James says, *"If they have sinned, they will be forgiven."* Sometimes a person is ill as a result of sin in their lives. This is especially true when you have experienced a great deal of pain in your life. Abandonment and abuse issues can be quite devastating and result in a sickness of the soul.

The answer, though, is not to keep it a secret between you and God; it is to tell an elder about your life. Tell him about the rape, the molestation, the abuse, and the rejection—then confess what it has done to you in terms of your sins. Tell him that the abuse, molestation, and abandonment has resulted in sexual sins—perhaps fornication, adultery, or homosexuality. It has caused you to be attracted to the wrong people. It has created ungodly soul ties in your life.

As you confess this to the elder, you will feel a great burden lifted off of you! The elder will declare to you, "Your sins are forgiven you!" Yes, you can confess this to God alone, and He will *forgive* you of your sins, but God wants to work through elders to *heal* you of your sins. You want more than forgiveness, you want healing, too. Healing comes through the *"prayer of a righteous man"* (James 5:16).

It is not a coincidence that James uses Elijah as an example of someone who called for a drought on Israel and then prayed for rain. *"Elijah was a human being, even as we are. He prayed earnestly that it would not rain, and it did not rain on the land for three and a half years. Again he prayed, and the heavens gave rain, and the earth produced its crops"* (James 5:17–18 NIV11).

Elijah saw the sins of Israel and retained their sins and thus *"prayed…that it would not rain."* Then, when Israel repented, he *"prayed, and the heavens gave rain."* James uses this illustration to show that, like Elijah, the elders can see your repentance and pray for healing. However, if you refuse to be honest with them, then they cannot pray for healing in your life. They will have no choice but to "retain your sins." Jesus said, *"Whose soever sins ye remit, they are remitted unto them; and whose soever sins ye retain, they are retained"* (John 20:23 KJV). This means that the sin remains on you. The elder can't lift off the ungodly soul ties and the addictive behavior because you were not honest in your confession. All the elder wants to hear in your confession is your honesty. Then he has no alternative but to forgive you—and he is happy to do so. Your sins get remitted, which means that they are erased from your life. They cannot influence you anymore. This forgiveness is God's forgiveness, which brings healing.

I have seen Christians struggle with sins—whether brought on by bad soul ties or not—and until they were willing to come to me or one of my elders to confess their sins, they could not be healed. But when they became humble and honest, God brought them healing. I wish I could give you a shorter route to your inner healing, but this is the only route you can take. It might be difficult, uncomfortable, or even painful, but I promise, it will be worth it.

ELEVEN

FORGIVE THOSE WHO HAVE HURT YOU

The famous actor, producer, and director Tyler Perry was in need of inner healing. As a child, he had received horrific beatings from his alcoholic father. One time, his father got the extension cord from the vacuum cleaner, and beat Tyler until the skin peeled off his back. At the age of ten, he was seduced by a friend's mother; later, he was sexually molested by another friend's father.

These experiences scarred him. As he became an adult, he had difficulty relating properly to men and women. Rumors circulated that he was gay. It wasn't that, though; it was that his painful upbringing as a child had left him confused. It was the sexual abuse that affected his ability to create good soul ties. At one point in his life, he even became homeless.

He looked like anything but a successful actor. Yet, despite the bad breaks in his life, he chose not to let them become an excuse. He persevered and became successful in Hollywood. He wasn't satisfied until he received the inner healing that Christ promises.

While filming the movie *Precious*, Perry had an epiphany: "I sat there in tears realizing that somehow, by the grace of God, I made it through. My tears were tears of joy, being thankful that I made it."[4] He credits God for helping him. According to Perry, the greatest truth that God used to heal him was that he needed to get rid of his bitterness. And his most important lesson was to learn to forgive!

FORGIVENESS IS FOR YOUR BENEFIT

Forgiving others who hurt you may be hard, but living with the pain is even harder. Jesus' main teaching was the need to forgive. Jesus taught that the person who does not forgive creates a prison for himself or herself, and they will not get out until they have paid the last penny of forgiveness. (See Matthew 5:25–26.)

Maybe you are paying for what others have done to you. Perhaps your parents abandoned you, and now you are paying for it by seeking parental figures who also take advantage of you. You were sexually abused, and now you are paying for it with sexual confusion and dissatisfaction. You were verbally abused by peers, and now you are paying for it with low self-esteem. You were hurt by a religious figure, and now you are paying for it with a lack of spiritual zeal.

---

4. Tyler Perry quoted in Michael Y. Park, "Tyler Perry Reveals He Was Abused as a Child," *People*, September 23, 2016, http://people.com/celebrity/tyler-perry-reveals-he-was-abused-as-a-child/ (accessed July 10, 2017).

I want to share with you a revelation that will open your eyes to forgiveness. The passage is from one of the most important chapters about God forgiving you:

> *If we claim to be without sin, we deceive ourselves and the truth is not in us. If we confess our sins, he is faithful and just and will forgive us our sins and purify us from all unrighteousness. If we claim we have not sinned, we make him out to be a liar and his word has no place in our lives. My dear children, I write this to you so that you will not sin. But if anybody does sin, we have one who speaks to the Father in our defense—Jesus Christ, the Righteous One. He is the atoning sacrifice for our sins, and not only for ours but also for the sins of the whole world.* (1 John 1:8–2:2)

There are two important truths that stand out in these verses.

1. IF YOU CLAIM TO BE WITHOUT SIN, YOU DECEIVE YOURSELF.

Many times, we judge others and forget to judge ourselves. It is easy to see the sins of others and forget that you have sinned as well. This deception can keep you in darkness.

Jesus told a story about two men, one a religious person and the other a greedy tax collector, who both went to the temple to pray. The first man prayed, "*God, I thank you that I am not like other people—robbers, evildoers, adulterers—or even like this tax collector. I fast twice a week and give a tenth of all I get*" (Luke 18:11–12 NIV11).

Notice the self-righteousness. Self-righteous people love to compare themselves to others. They believe they are not as bad as the other person. This attitude will keep you from inner healing because you will not truly forgive the people who hurt you. After all, you think you don't need much forgiveness. *I am not the problem*, you tell yourself. *They are the problem!*

Notice the prayer of the tax collector. He was so ashamed of himself that he would not even look up toward heaven. Instead, he beat his breasts, saying, *"God, have mercy on me, a sinner"* (verse 13 NIV11). Jesus said that the tax collector's prayer was more acceptable than the religious man's prayer. Why? Because he admitted that he was a sinner! The religious man, on the other hand, ignored his own sins, pointing his finger at the tax collector and focusing only on his good deeds.

YOU CANNOT REALLY CONFESS YOUR SINS TO GOD UNTIL YOU TRULY BELIEVE THAT YOU ARE A SINNER, AND THAT YOU NEED HIS MERCY DAILY.

You cannot really confess your sins to God until you truly believe that you are a sinner, and that you need His mercy daily. Don't focus on the sins of your parents, the rapist, the abuser, the cheating spouse, or the leaders who have fallen. Focus instead on your own need for mercy.

2. IF YOU CONFESS YOUR SIN TO GOD, HE WILL PURIFY YOU FROM THE CONTAMINATION OF OTHERS.

John doesn't simply say that if you confess your sins, God will cleanse you from the filth of your own sins. Rather, he said that God will *"purify us from all unrighteousness."* Not just your own unrighteousness, but even the unrighteousness of others.

You don't need to get the others to confess their sins for you to be purified from the contamination of their sins; you just need to confess your own sins.

You might question my interpretation of this passage, but notice what John says about the world's sins: "[Jesus] *is the atoning sacrifice for our sins, and not only for ours but also for the sins of the whole world*" (1 John 2:2).

Look, the truth is, Jesus died not just for your sins but also for the sins of the whole world. Now this is good news for you. You see, John was not saying that the whole world is presently forgiven. Of course, the world is not forgiven! Only God's children are forgiven, but the passage has great application for the contamination of your life by the sins of the world. Since Jesus died for the world's sins, this means that you can be released from the effects of the world's sins.

For example, you can be affected by the sins of your parents. God said that He would punish *"the children for the sin of the parents to the third and fourth generation of those who hate me, but show love to a thousand generations of those who love me and keep my commandments"* (Exodus 20:5–6 NIV11). As I was preaching this, the passage in 1 John came forcefully upon me. It hit me! The reason Jesus died for the sins of everyone was so that, first, all have the potential to be saved, but second, even if the people who sinned against you are not personally forgiven by God, they can be forgiven by you, because Jesus died for their sins. In other words, you might have to forgive people for their sins, even if God has not yet forgiven them of all their sins.

Jesus did this on the cross. He said, *"Father, forgive them, for they do not know what they are doing"* (Luke 23:34). God forgave all those responsible for crucifying Jesus, but this does not mean they were forgiven of all their sins, just the specific sin of crucifying Jesus. This means that God will not judge anyone for their part in crucifying Jesus, because Jesus forgave them and He asked God to forgive them. God has forgiven the people for crucifying Christ, yet only one person, the thief, entered heaven, because he confessed that Jesus was the King of kings when he asked Jesus to remember him when He came into His kingdom.

Not until a sinner acknowledges that Jesus is their Lord and King can they be saved and enter heaven. However, for the specific offense of crucifying Jesus, God forgave them.

LIKE CHRIST, YOU HAVE THE POWER TO FORGIVE SPECIFIC OFFENSES THAT PEOPLE HAVE DONE TO YOU. AND IN FORGIVING THEM OF THOSE OFFENSES, YOU ASK GOD TO FORGIVE THEM OF THOSE OFFENSES!

Like Christ, you have the power to forgive specific offenses that people have done to you. And in forgiving them of those offenses, you ask God to forgive them of those offenses! Ouch! You might say, "No, I want them to be punished for eternity for what they did to me." In that case, their sins are not forgiven, but neither are you free from the impurity of their offenses against you. You are still affected by their sins.

So when you forgive people for what they did to you, two things happen:

1. God forgives them.
2. God releases you from the impurities of their sins against you.

Now, it does not mean they will go to heaven without accepting Christ. Like the thief on the cross, they still need to accept Him. Yet, something very important happens to you: God releases you from the effects of their sins. The sickness in your soul, as a result of their sins against you, is healed.

A PRAYER FOR OFFENDERS

You cannot get healed of your sick soul without forgiving the offenders. So start your healing right now. Pray and forgive those who hurt you. Pray this:

> Father, in the name of Jesus, I see from your Word that I need mercy in the same way as those that hurt me. I will not be self-righteous and think that I am better than them. I need your mercy daily. So forgive me of anything that I have done that was displeasing to you. As you forgive me, I forgive others in the same way. Just as I want you to forgive me, I ask you to forgive those *who* hurt me (you might want to be specific and mention specific things people have done to you). I forgive ____________ for sinning against me when they ____________ me. I will not speak ill of them anymore. I completely, from my heart, forgive them!

The good news is that you don't have to pay for their sins anymore. In the next chapter, I will explain what you should do when you ask an elder to pray for inner healing in your life. I will also explain the role of the elder and what he or she must do to help you.

TWELVE

PRAY FOR INNER HEALING

You feel sick! Not physically, but emotionally. What is it? It is a broken soul. A broken soul will cause you to make terrible decisions in your life. David knew about those bad decisions. He wrote, *"Then I realized that my heart was bitter, and I was all torn up inside. I was so foolish and ignorant—I must have seemed like a senseless animal to you"* (Psalm 73:21–22 NLT).

Like him, you feel *"all torn up inside."* Life has dealt you one blow after another, and the result is that you *"seemed like a senseless animal."* You acted on instincts, rather than sane choices. You developed bonds with people who only hurt you more. You knew better, but that is what happens when you are torn up inside. It robs you of wisdom.

This is what happened to Annie Lobert. She never felt loved by her dad. This feeling of rejection led her to find love in all the wrong places. She made a terrible life choice by going into prostitution. As a prostitute, she met a man who was attractive and debonair. At first, he treated her nicely. He convinced her to move to Las Vegas where, he said, she could make a lot more money. After making the move, she discovered that he was involved in sex trafficking. He began to beat her if she complained about the underage girls he was forcing into prostitution. He would rape and beat her regularly, eventually forcing her to work for him in the sex industry. She felt trapped, but was afraid to leave.

The lifestyle was horrendous. She had post-traumatic stress disorder. She lost her appetite and developed anorexia. She feared getting fat, and had a lot of issues with her self-image. Despite her pimp's abuse, she also craved his attention. She gave him whatever he wanted; she was his slave.

Then one day, she suffered an apparent heart attack as a result of accidentally overdosing on drugs. It was in the midst of this crisis that she gave her life to Jesus. She escaped from her situation, and began to grow in the Lord. Eventually, she started Hookers of Jesus, a ministry that helps women in the sex industry to transition into a healthy, normal life.

Reporters have asked Annie if it really is possible to be psychologically healed from all that she went through, and she says yes. She offers the best key to inner healing, "The most important piece of healing is knowing that you're absolutely forgiven. That you are absolutely loved by God."[5]

Long before Annie started Hookers of Jesus, Jesus already had a ministry to women in the sex trade. Jesus ministered to

5. Angela Almeida, "Q&A with 'Hookers for Jesus' founder, Annie Lobert," MSNBC, June 26, 2015, http://www.msnbc.com/documentaries/q-hookers-jesus-founder-annie-lobert (accessed July 10, 2017).

them on at least two occasions. He even said to the chief priests and elders,

> *I tell you the truth, the tax collectors and the prostitutes are entering the kingdom of God ahead of you. For John came to you to show you the way of righteousness, and you did not believe him, but the tax collectors and the prostitutes did. And even after you saw this, you did not repent and believe him.* (Matthew 21:31–32)

THE ADULTEROUS WOMAN

The first woman He ministered to was the woman caught in the act of adultery. The religious leaders dragged her from the brothel: "*They made her stand before the group and said to Jesus, 'Teacher, this woman was caught in the act of adultery. In the Law Moses commanded us to stone such women. Now what do you say?'*" (John 8:3–5).

People often wonder why the man was not also dragged out to stand before the crowd. The reason is because in biblical times, adultery was an act of sex with a married person. The married person was not considered an adulterer unless he or she was having sex with someone else who was married. The woman was not married, but the man was. So he was considered a fornicator, but not an adulterer. There were no penalties for consensual, heterosexual fornication under the Old Testament, although it was still considered a sin.

How did Jesus bring her healing?

> *Jesus bent down and started to write on the ground with his finger. When they kept on questioning him, he straightened up and said to them, "If any one of you is without sin, let him be the first to throw a stone at her." Again he stooped down and wrote on the ground.* (verses 6–8)

What did Jesus write? Some have speculated that he was writing all the sins of the people. I believe that Jesus was actually writing out the Ten Commandments. Why do I believe this? First, Jesus wrote on the ground with *"his finger."* Not with a stick, but with His finger. This is the only place the Gospels record that Jesus ever wrote anything personally. He never wrote the Gospels or Letters. This is it!

Jesus is God, and there is one place in the Bible that says that God wrote something down personally, and it was the Ten Commandments. Moses was the witness: *"The LORD gave me two stone tablets inscribed by the finger of God"* (Deuteronomy 9:10). God used His *"finger"* to write the Ten Commandments. He did not use lightning or any natural instrument to write the commandments.

The second reason I believe that Jesus wrote the Ten Commandments is because He wrote twice. The Ten Commandments were on *"two stone tablets,"* so after Jesus wrote the first commandments that were on the first tablet, He stood up and said, *"If any one of you is without sin, let him be the first to throw a stone at her."* After these words, the Bible says, *"Again he stooped down and wrote on the ground"* (John 8:8). He stooped down again in order to write the commandments that were on the other tablet.

He was so absorbed in writing the Ten Commandments, that He was unaware of the people dropping their rocks and leaving. After they all left, the Bible says, *"Jesus straightened up and asked her, 'Woman, where are they? Has no one condemned you?' 'No one, sir,' she said"* (verses 10–11).

The people got the point. They had been focused on the one command against adultery, but forgot the rest of God's commands. Even if they had not committed adultery, they had broken other commands, such as honoring their mother and father. Which of them could honestly say that they had always respected their parents? Surely, everyone has at one time spoken disrespectful words to their parents.

The message is clear: all are sinners. Whether you are a prostitute or a vanilla type of sinner, you are still a sinner who needs God's grace and mercy.

This is what Jesus gave to the woman: "'*Then neither do I condemn you,' Jesus declared. 'Go now and leave your life of sin*'" (John 8:11).

TO EXPERIENCE INNER HEALING, YOU MUST ACCEPT GOD'S MERCY AND GRACE. GOD DOES NOT OFFER GRACE AFTER YOU CHANGE, HE OFFERS IT BEFORE YOU CHANGE.

To experience inner healing, you must accept God's mercy and grace. God does not offer grace after you change, He offers it before you change. It is the grace of God that will change you, not your good deeds.

Paul affirmed this: "*Or do you show contempt for the riches of his kindness, tolerance and patience, not realizing that God's kindness leads you toward repentance?*" (Romans 2:4). Paul reminds the "rock throwers" that God changed them with kindness, not with the law.

The woman caught in adultery could not change unless God first forgave her. God forgives you first, then He calls you to change. Don't ever think God has stopped forgiving you because you have not changed enough! God still forgives because He knows you will stop sinning eventually, but He will never stop forgiving you. You will never receive inner healing if you think it is dependent upon your change. No! Your inner healing is dependent upon your acceptance of God's forgiveness for your sins.

YOU WILL NEVER RECEIVE INNER HEALING IF YOU THINK IT IS DEPENDENT UPON YOUR CHANGE. NO! YOUR INNER HEALING IS DEPENDENT UPON YOUR ACCEPTANCE OF GOD'S FORGIVENESS FOR YOUR SINS.

Jesus said, *"If any one of you is without sin, let him be the first to throw a stone at her."* As a broken person, you could easily make the mistake of taking up rocks and stoning the people who hurt you, but you cannot expect God to heal your heart while stoning the perpetrators of your pain. Like them, you also have hurt others—you are not without sin. You cannot receive healing in your soul while maintaining bitterness in your heart. You must forgive the people who have hurt you: forgive your father and mother; forgive your brothers and sisters; forgive your friends; forgive your spouse; forgive the minister; forgive the rapist and abusers. Yes, forgive them all!

Another thing Jesus told the woman was "Go *now and leave your life of sin.*" He did not say, "Stop committing adultery!"

That is obviously included, but Jesus expands it to her whole life, telling her to leave her life of sin. Jesus was not concerned only for her career, but her existence! Jesus cares about your life; not just one sin in your life. He was calling the woman to wholeness, and He calls you to wholeness, too.

The Greek is emphatic. It reads, "Immediately, stop missing the mark." There is something you can do right now! Stop sinning; stop the adultery; stop the abuse; stop the lies. You don't have to wait until you feel real good to stop doing whatever is hurting you. Stop now!

MARY MAGDALENE

The second woman that Jesus ministered to was Mary Magdalene. It is traditionally believed that Mary was the woman washing Jesus' feet in Luke 7.

> *Now one of the Pharisees invited Jesus to have dinner with him, so he went to the Pharisee's house and reclined at the table. When a woman who had lived a sinful life in that town learned that Jesus was eating at the Pharisee's house, she brought an alabaster jar of perfume, and as she stood behind him at his feet weeping, she began to wet his feet with her tears. Then she wiped them with her hair, kissed them and poured perfume on them. When the Pharisee who had invited him saw this, he said to himself, "If this man were a prophet, he would know who is touching him and what kind of woman she is—that she is a sinner."* (Luke 7:36–39)

Mary was not invited to the dinner. She crashed the dinner-party in order to get close to Jesus and worship Him with repentance. Feeling ashamed for her sins, she wept. She noticed that the host did not provide a wash basin and cloth to clean Jesus' feet, so she used her own tears and hair to bathe them.

She could not stop crying! She could not stop following Jesus. He went to His seat, and Mary continued to wash His feet. Simon, the host and Pharisee, probably had some choice thoughts about this situation. *Why does Jesus allow this woman to touch him? She is filthy! He should kick her out of my house! Yet He gets some sort of delight in the affection of this prostitute. I highly doubt He is a holy man of God!*

His eyes gave away his disdain for the woman and for Jesus, so Jesus interrupted his chain of thoughts: *"Simon, I have something to tell you."* Startled, Simon replied, *"Tell me, teacher"* (Luke 7:40).

IT'S NOT FAITH IN OPTIMISM THAT SAVES YOU; IT'S FAITH IN GOD'S GRACE AND MERCY!

Jesus told a story to illustrate that if you are forgiven much, you love much. He pointed out that Simon had not treated Jesus as an important guest, yet this woman had treated Him like God. She had sinned much, therefore she loved Jesus that much more Then Jesus shocked everyone in the room: *"Jesus said to her, 'Your sins are forgiven.' The other guests began to say among themselves, 'Who is this who even forgives sins?' Jesus said to the woman, 'Your faith has saved you; go in peace'"* (verses 48–50).

Like the woman caught in adultery, Jesus forgave Mary before she officially quit her lifestyle. Notice, however, that she did offer one act of repentance: her tears. That was enough!

Can you give God your tears of repentance? That's all He wants for now!

He told her that her faith saved her. What faith? Faith in Jesus' mercy! It's not faith in optimism that saves you; it's faith in God's grace and mercy!

She treated Jesus as God, and so He forgave her as God! Is that how you view Jesus? He is God; He is the one who can forgive you and heal your inner wounds.

THE BROKEN HEART

Jesus' main mission was to heal broken hearts. Listen to His inaugural sermon at Nazareth:

> *And there was delivered unto him the book of the prophet Esaias. And when he had opened the book, he found the place where it was written, The Spirit of the Lord is upon me, because he hath anointed me to preach the gospel to the poor; he hath sent me to heal the brokenhearted, to preach deliverance to the captives, and recovering of sight to the blind, to set at liberty them that are bruised, to preach the acceptable year of the Lord.* (Luke 4:17–19 KJV)

Jesus took no time finding the passage. He knew it was about Him. This is why He had been anointed by God in the River Jordan. He was sent to "*heal the brokenhearted.*" There is no worse disease than a broken heart.

No wonder Jesus spent an inordinate amount of time with prostitutes. He knew that among them, the brokenhearted were to be found.

The passage in Isaiah was taken from Isaiah 61. The Hebrew word for "brokenhearted" is *shabar.* It means "to burst, to break down, to break into pieces, to crush, to destroy, to tear, and to hurt." Does that describe you?

Jesus is the only one anointed by God to heal you. Psychiatrists without Christ are incapable of healing you. You might have sought help from professionals—God bless them—but unless you let the Lord heal you, you will remain sick in your soul. The answer is Christ. The reason He can heal you is because He is the One who took on your pain at the cross. Others may sympathize with your pain, and offer you excellent guidance and temporary relief from pain, but Jesus is the only One who literally and actually took it from you at the cross.

OTHERS MAY SYMPATHIZE WITH YOUR PAIN, AND OFFER YOU EXCELLENT GUIDANCE AND TEMPORARY RELIEF FROM PAIN, BUT JESUS IS THE ONLY ONE WHO LITERALLY AND ACTUALLY TOOK IT FROM YOU AT THE CROSS.

Also, only Jesus has always been with you. No human has always been with you. He has seen your life in a way that others could never understand. Jesus also takes the place of the people who should have been there for you but were not. God told the widows, *"Do not be afraid; you will not be put to shame. Do not fear disgrace; you will not be humiliated. You will forget the shame of your youth and remember no more the reproach of your widowhood. For your Maker is your husband"* (Isaiah 54:4–5).

God can be your father and mother. He can be your brother and sister. He can be your husband or wife. In other words, He will take the place of the absentees in your life.

Jesus is also with you always. He says, "I will never leave you nor forsake you. And surely I am with you always, to the very end of the age." (See Deuteronomy 31:6; Matthew 28:20.)

This reminds me of a little boy who walked home with his mother during a furious lightning storm. Every time a flash of lightning struck the sky, the little boy would stop to look up and smile. He did this throughout the entire walk to home, stopping at least a dozen times. After getting out of the storm, his mother asked, "Why did you keep stopping and smiling at the sky every time there was a flash of lightning?"

The little boy replied, "Because God was taking my picture."

YOU MAY HAVE THOUGHT THAT GOD WAS FAR AWAY WHEN YOU WERE HURT, BUT HE WASN'T. HE HAS BEEN WITH YOU THROUGH IT ALL. KNOWING THIS IS A VITAL STEP TO YOUR INNER HEALTH.

The child has it right. Every time there was a terrible storm in your life, God pictured you in His mind. He remembers the pain you felt. It is embedded in His mind. He has not forgotten what you looked like when you were hurt. You may have thought that God was far away when you were hurt, but He wasn't. He has been with you through it all. Knowing this is a vital step to your inner health.

PRAYER FOR INNER HEALING

I have traveled the world, and I have been an eyewitness to God's grace in healing the sick soul. I was there praying for Ruth, the woman who had been molested by her father, while the MSNBC producers filmed it all. The power of God to heal was so strong that the producers shed tears. Today, I want to offer to pray for you. While I am not there in person, I am going to do my best in lead you in a prayer for inner healing. If possible, it would be better if an elder of your church could lead you in this prayer. Maybe they could read the prayer first and then guide you.

Here is what I want you to do.

First, get alone with God, and maybe a church elder or two. You don't want to pray this prayer in front of the public—it's too emotional.

Second, as I lead you in the prayer, I will insert instructions in parentheses, which will ask you to do something. Please do it. Don't be too quick to rush through the prayer. Don't skip the instructions.

Now, I want you to get on your knees. You might use a pillow to support your weight. If you have bad knees, then sit. Show humility to God. Pray these words:

> Dear heavenly Father, I come to you not on my own merits, but on the merit of Jesus Christ. You know me. You saw my unformed body fashioned in my mother's womb. You gave me the parents that I have. I do not complain about my life.
>
> **CONFESSION:** First, I want to confess to You my sins.
>
> *(At this point, confess your sins to God and to the elder. Be specific. Even if you are embarrassed to let the elder hear you, say it anyway.)*

ADMISSION: You know how broken I feel. My heart has been crushed.

(Tell God all the times you were crushed by others. Be specific. Take your time.)

TRUTH: Through it all, the devil has lied to me by telling me that I was alone. I have not been alone. You have been with me though all these times.

(Now visualize the truth that God has been with you during all those bad moments. For example, visualize that God was holding your hand while you were being molested. Visualize that God had walked with you when your parents were not there for you. Visualize God sitting down with you at the dinner table while your husband left you for someone else.)

FORGIVE: You said in Your Word that for me to be forgiven, I must forgive. This is what I will do now. I ask You to forgive the people who have hurt me.

(Be specific and describe what each person did to you and then, after describing what they did, ask God to forgive them.)

As I ask You to forgive them, I also forgive them.

(Say who you forgive and what you forgive them for. At this point, you may be weeping. Take your time.)

ASK: Now Jesus, the Father anointed You to heal the brokenhearted. See this heart of mine; it's broken. Please, Jesus, heal my heart now!"

(If an elder is there, the elder should lay hands on you, and ask God to heal your heart. Continue to kneel and let the elder pray for you. The elder should give any words from the Holy Spirit to give comfort or direction to you.)

You should feel your heart being healed. Let Jesus do it. You might be weeping, much like Mary Magdalene—that's okay. The weeping is good for you; it cleanses you from the contamination of your spirit.

If you are not a very emotional person, then you may not have wept during this prayer. That's okay, too. The woman caught in adultery did not weep, either. Everyone is different. But please believe that Jesus Christ is healing your heart.

On the other hand, if you felt no emotions whatsoever, and you prayed this on your own, then it is a sure sign that you need to confess to an elder and have them pray for you. You need accountability and a human component.

You must accept by faith that God is healing your heart. Believe that you are being changed! Don't accept the old you anymore. You are a new person!

PART V
HOW TO HANDLE REJECTION

THIRTEEN

MY BATTLE WITH REJECTION

The scene seemed so serene. My wife, Sonia, and I had just finished conducting a two-day retreat near Bonita Lake, a deserved name. It was a beautiful waterside retreat. Along with a few other church members, we had driven to the lake to admire the shimmering waters. While others talked about the lake, my wife and I kept quiet. We had plastered smiles on our faces so that none of the attendees would notice our sadness. Little did they know about the serious discussion my wife and I had while driving there.

"I want to give up!"

"I want to leave my church!"

"I'm tired of pastoring."

"I'm ready to quit."

Sonia could not believe these words had come pouring out of my mouth.

I had always seemed to be someone who has had his act together. I seemed invincible. People had admired my strong persistence and faith and how God had used me in mighty ways. I had built a large church. Thousands had been saved through my ministry, and hundreds more had been healed—some miraculously. Incredible results had been the norm.

Lately, though, not much was happening. The church was stagnant. Some long-time members had left. I was told by one of those families that our church "wasn't spiritual enough" for them. Others had followed their lead. I felt that a mass exodus was just around the corner.

In the midst of this crisis, a lake retreat seemed just what our church needed. So several families from our church joined us for this time of refreshment—at least, I thought it would be refreshing. But by the last service on Sunday morning, half of the people stayed in their rooms and tents. They weren't spiritual enough to come to Sunday morning worship at the retreat.

Why are they so indifferent to Christ? I wondered. *The answer must be me. I'm the problem. That family was right, our church isn't spiritual enough, and I am the problem. I'm at fault.*

Sonia, knowing I was serious about leaving, not just our church but the ministry, wept. "You can't quit. You're needed."

"I'm not needed. I'm hurting the church. What they need is a new pastor."

Nothing my helpmate said could change my mind. I was determined to quit. The thought of giving up did not settle well with me, though; I knew deep inside that this was not the answer. But I didn't know what else to do, and I didn't want to keep living this way.

We arrived home early that evening. My wife went to bed, and I sat alone in the living room with nothing to do but watch TV.

I might as well turn on Pastor John Osteen, I thought. *Now that's a good pastor. Oh, if only our churches had someone like John Osteen, then I know they would grow fast.*

Not too long into his message, Pastor Osteen stopped, turned toward the camera, and pointed his finger at it. That finger seemed to reach out of my television set. With his trademark, gravelly voice, boldly and compassionately, he said, "I'm talking to a pastor who is ready to give up his church. You didn't have a good Sunday service. You're thinking about quitting. You believe that you're not the man for the job. But you *are* the man for the job. There's not a better man for your church but you. Don't quit!"

I sat there stunned. I could not hold back the tears. I burst.

Could I really be the man for the job? But I'm exhausted. Oh wait, I'm not exhausted because I'm overworked. I'm exhausted for another reason altogether. But why am I so tired? Why do I want to give up?

The next morning, I told my wife about what John Osteen had said. She was thrilled; I was too. Well, sort of. I needed more answers. Why was I feeling so tired?

Before long, God broke through. He spoke to me in a very clear voice—so clear, it was almost audible. The message He gave me was about to radically change my attitude. The attitude I had concerning everything, not just church and ministry, but every aspect of my life. Since receiving that message, I haven't been the same. I have been filled almost constantly with joy, and that joy has spilled over into my church. My countenance is improved; I'm happy. This does not mean I have not experienced rejection, because I have, but now I know how I am supposed to handle it.

IF YOU DO NOT KNOW HOW TO HANDLE REJECTION, IT WILL BREAK YOUR HEART AND CAUSE YOU TO FORM NEW AND UNGODLY SOUL TIES.

If you do not know how to handle rejection, it will break your heart and cause you to form new and ungodly soul ties. My goal in this section of the book is to help you learn to handle rejection. Unless you learn how to do this, you will remain susceptible to the same ungodly soul ties I experienced.

What was it that God showed me that changed my life? Let me tell you.

THE ENEMY

The greatest battle I faced in the ministry was not a battle against finances or illness. My toughest battle was with rejection. I never thought rejection would be the enemy that almost beat me.

Ten years prior to the crisis at Bonita Lake, I had entered the ministry with excitement. I could hardly wait to win souls for the Lord. It did not bother me that some people who came to church did not want to accept the Lord. I did not take that personally.

Ironically, the ones who hurt me the most were those who had already accepted the Lord, had become filled with the Spirit, had allowed me to baptize them, and then joined my church. I saw their families and friends come to the Lord also. I married some of them. I performed funerals for their loved ones. I counseled them in times of trouble. I went to their birthday parties. These people were more than members; they were friends. Yet they would be the ones who hurt me most when they left.

It's inevitable that people leave for one reason or another. But when several families that were close friends decided to leave together, it was more than I could handle. This was the most difficult battle of my life. The rejection hurt so badly, I wanted to leave the ministry.

The worst part of being a pastor is not the lack of money or privacy. It's not even the midnight calls for prayer. The hardest part of the job, for me at least, is the pain of rejection. I hate to be rejected by others. If most pastors are honest, they, too, would agree that rejection is the worst part of the ministry.

The saddest part was that I wasn't equipped to face the battle of rejection. No one told me how to deal with rejection.

REJECTION IS COMMON

Pastors are not the only ones who face rejection. It is something everyone faces. You have faced it. It hurts, doesn't it?

Perhaps, when you were in elementary school, you were always picked last to play on the softball team. You cringed when it was time for the captains to pick the players they wanted on their teams. You knew that you were going to be chosen last. Every time they mentioned someone else's name, it felt like a dagger was piercing your heart. You swallowed the pain of rejection. Finally, your name was called. You bowed your head, tucked your glove under your arm, and trotted out to right field. The captain would yell at you, "Further back! Back more! More!" You were so far back, you felt like you might as well jump over the fence and go home.

I was always fairly athletic. I was often the team captain, or, at the very least, one of the first picks. But I'll never forget one day when I was trying out for a basketball team. Two years prior to that, I had been first-string on our school team. Now, however, I was trying out for a new team, one which combined players from three of the best schools in the area.

Finally, the time came on that fateful evening when the coach pulled out the roster and named all the kids who had made the team. I listened for my name, but it was never called. The coach folded up the roster, looked at us, and said, "For those whose name wasn't mentioned, I want to say, 'Thank you for trying.' You can go home."

My friends who had made the team gathered around and said, "Alright, with all those losers gone, we can really start to play."

One of the guys threw me the ball and said, "C'mon, let's play."

I held the ball in my hand, not knowing what to do. Then one of the guys asked, "What's wrong, Tom?"

I could hardly tell him, "I…I…uh…I did not make the team."

"No way! The coach made a mistake." The guys went to talk with the coach.

A few minutes later, the coach walked up to me and said, "I was just joking. Of course you made the team." *Relief.* But I'll never forget the pain I felt in my chest as I held back the tears. It was horrible.

THE PAIN OF DIVORCE

Divorce is probably the worst rejection pain someone can go through, especially when it's your spouse, not you, who chooses to leave. Perhaps he or she left you for someone else. It hurts so much, you feel like you can't go on. You want to hide from everyone. You begin to question your self-worth. *What's wrong with me? What did I do wrong? If only I was a better spouse.*

Russell Reese knows the pain of divorce. He described:

> I came home one evening, and she was gone. The hours passed, and she just never came home. There had been no mention of divorce, no notes, no phone calls. She had just vanished, and had taken the kids with her.... The next few days, weeks, and months, turned into a living hell. The most important thing in my life had walked out the door. My family!
>
> I found myself sitting alone, bewildered and forlorn. I found myself abandoned, alone, with feelings of rejection, dejection, and despair. I found myself desolated, *disconnected,* and disjoined, from everything that I had valued in life. I was depressed and distraught, as my whole outlook on life had become disoriented and distorted.... There are not words enough in our language, *to* accurately describe how I felt. It was like I was living in a black hole, *and there was* no place to run, nowhere to hide.... Life, as I had known it was over. *I had been double-crossed, dishonored, and demeaned. I had been victimized. MY WIFE HAD FILED FOR DIVORCE!*
>
> *Why would she do such a thing?*[6]

6. Russell Reese, *Divorce: The Devil's Battleground* (Christian Ebook Publisher, 2011).

The questions never seem to end. Your self-esteem is at an all-time low.

I suppose the worst case of rejection was the man who sent his application along with a picture of himself to the Lonely Hearts Club, only to receive a letter two weeks later that said, "We're not that lonely!"

Okay, that one was a joke.

Real rejection, however, is not funny. Throughout life, we all will face rejection. It comes in many forms: parents favoring another sibling, your boss calling you in to fire you, friends not showing up to your wedding, etc. When it happens, you take it personally.

Some of you may have even experienced rejection from the time you were born. You were abandoned or felt unwanted by your parents.

Perhaps even at church, you still feel unwelcome, and now, you just don't want to expose yourself to any more hurt. I know how you feel.

WATCH OUT FOR THAT GRINGO

My problem with rejection goes back to when I was in school. On the first day of junior high, as I left the house to walk to school, terrible thoughts hit my mind. I now realize that they were demonic thoughts, but at the time, I didn't recognize them as devilish. *What if you go to lunch and no one wants to eat with you? You will be by yourself. You will look foolish. People will talk about you.*

These thoughts haunted me all through the morning. Finally, the lunch bell rang. *What am I going to do?* I was so scared of being rejected that I walked home to eat. From that day on, I ate at home, always afraid that I would not have any friends.

I actually experienced the painful side of prejudice in my freshman year of high school. Although I now ate in the cafeteria (I had to because I went to school on a bus), I still suffered from rejection. The high school I attended was a half-mile from the border of Mexico. Consequently, most of the students were Hispanic.

Now, I am familiar with Hispanics. My wife is Hispanic. My grandfather was half-Hispanic, so I'm part Hispanic myself, but you would be hard-pressed to see the Hispanic blood in me. My surname may be Brown, but I look white.

In my biology class there was a big, husky guy named Arturo. He was a star football player, and everyone looked up to him. For some reason, he had it in for me. One day in class, he stood up, pointed at me, and said, "Everyone listen to me. You see this gringo? He's our enemy. If anyone chooses to be his friend, you become an enemy of our people!"

This guy didn't even know who I was. I had never spoken a cross word to him, yet he hated me, I assume, because I was white. At that moment, I felt isolated, alone. I wanted to crawl under my desk and disappear. I never felt the same again. I would go home and be in a rage with this guy. I envisioned killing him. The only thing that stopped me was his size.

Toward the end of the school year, I sought help from a school counselor. Once I was in his office, the counselor asked, "What can I do for you?"

I didn't know how to say it. I squirmed, fidgeted with my shoestrings, and then I could hold it back no longer. I burst into tears. "I don't want to come back to this school! The people hate me because I'm white. Please transfer me to another school. I can't take it another year. Please help me get out of this school!" He did.

FRUITS OF REJECTION

King Saul felt rejected when the people began to sing the song, *"Saul has slain his thousands, and David his tens of thousands"* (1 Samuel 18:7). How did Saul react? He began to throw spears at David.

I made the same mistake. When people began to leave my church, I began to attack the members who stayed. Instead of treating them with love and kindness, I took out my feelings of hurt and betrayal on them. I became a meaner preacher. My messages had an edge to them, and people could sense that something was wrong with me. The first obvious fruit of rejection is *anger*.

This calls to mind the story of a man who was fired from his job. As he drove recklessly home, the police pulled him over and gave him a ticket. Then his radiator overheated. When he finally arrived home, he found his mailbox knocked down. On top of that, the doorknob was stuck. When he walked into the house, he tripped over the carpet, his wife was late with dinner, and the children were sick—everything was going wrong for this man. Finally, his faithful cat walked over to him and affectionately rubbed his leg with her chin and purred. The man looked down in anger and kicked the cat.

Let me ask you something: who have you been kicking? I was kicking my church members, the very people who loved and supported me. This of course led to more people leaving the church. After all, who wants to stay and be pastored by an angry preacher? The more people left, the meaner I became. I was driving people away, and had no idea why I was doing it.

The second thing I did was refuse to allow people to get close to me. I didn't want to spend time with friends, because then they might leave me as well. I was pushing away the good soul ties because of my feelings of rejection. You might be doing that, too.

My self-esteem was in the tank. I couldn't believe that people still wanted to stay and let me be their pastor. I expected everyone to leave and find someone else who could do a better job than I could. I was also afraid to confront people with real sins. I did not want to risk their rejection. If I told them to repent, I reasoned, they might find another church that would accept them as they were, and then I would be worse off than before!

Fear gripped me; I might lose my church. Soon, I panicked—there would not even be enough money to continue the ministry.

I was experiencing the classic fruits of rejection: anger, fear of intimacy, loss of self-esteem, fear of confrontation, and the fear of failure.

Have you been experiencing the same fruits?

FOURTEEN

THE PRAYER GOD COULDN'T ANSWER

I thank God for the encouraging words of John Osteen. Maybe, as he said, I *was* the pastor for my church, but I still needed a personal revelation from God if I was to continue. The answer came in an unexpected way.

My wife had asked me to get some groceries at the store. As I drove there, the Lord opened my mind to the work of the enemy. Satan was using a weapon on me that I hadn't detected: the weapon of rejection. Never before had I seen Satan's plot like I was seeing it this time. Oh, I had seen Satan afflict people with illnesses, rob people of finances, and tear marriages apart, but I never realized what he was doing to me. I was blind.

In my car, the Lord made me confront the greatest fear I had ever faced—the dread of rejection. It was a weakness that I had never admitted. I was frightened of it. Then God gave me a revelation on how to handle rejection. Here is the message He gave me.

YOU'RE NOT ALONE

First, He began to show me that *everyone* gets rejected. No one is immune to it. There is a certain comfort in knowing that you are not alone. It's even more comforting to know that everyone has experienced what you are experiencing. Rejection is a human condition. You are not human if you have not been rejected. I felt consoled when I grasped the fact that every pastor has been rejected. No one is exempt. Not one!

Preachers shout *Amen!* when they hear other pastors talk about all the new members they have received into their churches. But often, a part of them feels even worse after hearing those wonderful testimonies, because instead of rejoicing in the pastor's victories, they only recall their own failures. *What is he doing right that I have failed to do?* Thoughts like that haunt pastors.

This reminds me of a minister's conference I attended. Tommy Barnett, pastor of one of America's largest churches, spoke about all the wonderful outreaches that his congregation was doing. He talked about the hundred-plus ministries in his church. He spoke about the tens of thousands of people who attended his Easter pageants. Thousands more were fed thanksgiving meals. His church was bursting at the seams.

The following night at the conference, the next speaker softly said, "Well, I was going to brag to you about the three new families we added last Sunday, but after hearing from Tommy Barnett, I've changed my mind."

Don't misunderstand me—we should celebrate the positive testimonies of other ministers, and, hopefully, learn from them and be encouraged. But at the same time, the human side of us would like to hear about the struggles other ministers are facing, not so that we can have a pity party, but so that we don't feel we are the only ones facing struggle.

God began to show me that every minister, no matter how big his church, has also faced rejection. No one is so good that they have dodged it.

GOOD PEOPLE FEEL REJECTED

Next, the Lord clearly showed me that even *good* people face rejection. The Bible is filled with heroes who were rejected: Job, Joseph, and Paul, to name a few. They were not bad people, yet they were rejected.

Job was a great man, yet he went through trouble that eventually caused his friends to reject and malign him. Job was better than his friends, but he was rejected by them.

Joseph was the favorite son of Jacob. He was a good son, yet his brothers hated him and sold him as a slave. He did not deserve that treatment. Good people do not deserve to be mistreated, but they often are.

Paul was thrown into prison numerous times, simply for preaching the gospel. He was rejected for doing good.

Until I was rejected, I had never questioned my work, but now I was constantly analyzing. *Maybe I did something bad to deserve such rejection,* I wondered. The Lord, however, convinced me that I had not done anything to deserve rejection. It was not totally my fault that people were leaving my church. I was still doing what God considered to be good.

As I contemplated these truths, I immediately remembered the Scriptures about Jesus, the only perfect One. Even He was rejected.

> *As you come to him, the living Stone—rejected by men but chosen by God and precious to him.* (1 Peter 2:4)

> *He was in the world, and though the world was made through him, the world did not recognize him. He came to that which was his own, but his own did not receive him.* (John 1:10–11)

> *He grew up before him like a tender shoot, and like a root out of dry ground. He had no beauty or majesty to attract us to him, nothing in his appearance that we should desire him. He was despised and rejected by mankind, a man of sorrows, and familiar with suffering. Like one from whom men hide their faces he was despised, and we esteemed him not.* (Isaiah 53:2–3)

Jesus was rejected! If He was rejected, how could I expect to be accepted by everyone? If people rejected Him, then they are going to reject me. Jesus said, "*Remember the words I spoke to you: 'No servant is greater than his master.' If they persecuted me, they will persecute you also*" (John 15:20). No matter how perfect a pastor I could ever be, I would still be rejected—there's no way around it.

I finally accepted the fact that my rejection was not because something was wrong with me. God still accepted me. "*To the praise of the glory of his grace, wherein he hath made us accepted in the beloved*" (Ephesians 1:6 KJV). I was accepted in Him and I was pleasing to the Father despite the rejection of others. That was a load off my shoulders!

So I prayed. "Alright Lord, I understand that everyone has been rejected, even good people. I understand that! Jesus was perfect, yet He was rejected. I realize that I will always experience rejection. I accept it as a part of life. But, Lord, since this is my lot in life, please, take away the pain I feel when people reject me. Don't let me get hurt. Don't let me feel pain. Let me be able to brush off the rejection, so that it doesn't grieve me."

I fully expected the Lord to instantly heal me from the pain I felt. Instead, He shocked me. He said, "I'm sorry, I can't answer your prayer."

"What? I simply asked You to remove the pain and sorrow I feel when I'm rejected."

"But, Tom, you are asking Me to do something for you that is not Christ-like."

And then it hit me. *"He was despised and rejected by mankind, a man of suffering"* (Isaiah 53:3). Even Jesus felt sorrow when people rejected Him. It's Christ-like to feel sorrow when people reject you.

EVEN JESUS FELT SORROW WHEN PEOPLE REJECTED HIM. IT'S CHRIST-LIKE TO FEEL SORROW WHEN PEOPLE REJECT YOU.

Do you understand what God would have to do to take away sorrow when people reject you? He would have to stop you from caring for people. After all, why do you feel hurt when you get rejected? You hurt because you love the people who rejected you. To stop hurting is to stop loving.

I realized that in order to avoid the pain, I would have to avoid caring for and loving my congregation, and that was totally out of the question. As I considered God's response to my prayer, I realized that it was the people I loved the most who had hurt me the most. Only someone close to me could hurt me that much.

Many people visit my church. I don't know who they are because many of them never come back. I don't get hurt because I don't really have any feelings toward them. They're strangers. In the same way, sometimes a stranger yells obscenities to me while I'm driving. I don't get upset because they are strangers. I don't know who they are, and I don't really have affection for them, so I don't cry over them. But the people I love can hurt me deeply.

As God began to unfold this truth to me in my car, I realized how much I loved the people who left my church. This is why I was hurt. But I couldn't stop the pain, because I still loved them. For me to stop hurting meant I had to stop loving them. And I was not going to stop loving them. So I had to accept the sorrow as being from God. God is love, and my sorrow stemmed from love.

Tears began to stream down my cheeks. I told the Lord, "I see it. I'm glad I hurt, because it shows that I love those who have rejected me."

To hurt because of love is not the same as a sick soul. In fact, it is a sign of a healthy soul. Do not confuse the need for inner healing with the love you feel for people when you lose them.

JESUS' OWN TEARS

Then the Lord began to tell me about His own tears.

I was sobbing in my car as Jesus showed me His pain of rejection. I saw Jesus climbing a hill that overlooked Jerusalem. I pictured Him staring at that ancient city. He remembered all the prophets who tried to turn the people back to God. Jesus pondered the fate of the city. He grieved over the callousness of the religious leaders. Tears filled His eyes and He could take it no more. He fell down on His knees, and He began to weep over His own people. His eyes wet the ground with tears as He sobbed for what seemed like an eternity.

Finally, He spoke: *"O Jerusalem, Jerusalem, you who kill the prophets and stone those sent to you, how often I have longed to gather your children together, as a hen gathers her chicks under her wings, but you were not willing"* (Matthew 23:37).

Jesus knew the sorrow that comes from rejection. He felt it; it hurt.

The shortest verse in the Bible is John 11:35: *"Jesus wept."* One translation says, *"Jesus burst into tears"* (MOFFATT).

Who was He crying over—some stranger? No, He was crying over a friend, Lazarus. His tears did not go unnoticed. The people around Him exclaimed, *"See how he loved him!"* (verse 36).

The more you love, the more you will cry. It's a law; that's the way it works.

So your husband left you. You cry, and you try to tell yourself that you don't care, but you do care. Why? Because you still love him. You can't deny it, and you shouldn't. You should let your love move you to pray for him. When you do, you are acting like Christ. If he returns, you can forgive as Christ would.

I wanted to stop crying over those who left my church, but I couldn't because I still loved them. The more I contemplated the sorrow of Christ, the more I realized that it was Christ-like for me to weep. I loved those members. I wanted them back.

Okay, pastor, your sheep left you. Stop trying to "get over" those members. It hurts; it should. If it doesn't hurt, you have stopped loving them. Always love them; pray for them; rejoice when they come back. If they don't come back, love them anyway.

Many pastors try to convince themselves that they don't need those members. "No big deal. So they left. I don't need them. I'll do better without them." What kind of attitude is that? That's not Christ-like. That's hurt talking, not Christ talking.

Jesus didn't look over Jerusalem and say, "No big deal. Who cares about this city? There are other cities that will accept Me. I'll go to them. Forget Jerusalem!" No! God can't forget Jerusalem. He promises to come back for her, again. In fact, the Bible says that Jesus will return to Jerusalem—the very place that crucified Him. Jesus has not forgotten her. He still loves her to this day.

Paul, himself, prayed,

> *I have great sorrow and unceasing anguish in my heart. For I could wish that I myself were cursed and cut off from Christ for the sake of my brothers, those of my own race, the people of Israel.... My heart's desire and prayer to God for the Israelites is that they may be saved.*
>
> (Romans 9:2–4; 10:1)

Paul's heart was not callous. Sure, he could have become bitter toward his own people for the way they treated him, but he still loved them, and wanted them to come to the Lord. This is the way Christ acted.

How are you acting toward those who have rejected you? Are you angry with them? Are you looking to get even? Do you pretend that you don't care?

REJECTION BEFORE ACCEPTANCE

I'm not saying you should be a sobbing mess all the time. You also should not become hard-hearted. At the same time, after you've cried, you need to move on. Some of the people who left you were not godly soul ties. Some of the people *were* godly soul ties, and you can't stop loving them. But you cannot get stuck in past relationships; you must move on.

Jesus did not get stuck in Jerusalem. He reached out to the world; He told His disciples to go to Jerusalem, Judea, Samaria, and to the uttermost parts of the world. (See Acts 1:8.) In other words, don't forget Jerusalem—in fact, begin there—but remember you need to move on and realize that there is a big old world out there that needs Jesus.

Paul knew it was time to move on. He said, *"From now on I will go to the Gentiles"* (Acts 18:6). Paul was not foolish enough to keep extending his hands to the same people who kept rejecting his message. He moved on to the Gentiles and had great success with them.

Jesus said, *"If anyone will not welcome you or listen to your words, shake the dust off your feet when you leave that home or town"* (Matthew 10:14). Do not misinterpret this to mean that we should become angry, vowing never to return. To *"shake the dust off your feet"* is an old term meaning to move on, to go forward.

There are so many people who refuse to go forward. For example, many divorced people live in the past. They refuse to get over their broken marriages, they keep fighting with their ex-spouses, and they refuse to let them get on with their lives. Their eyes are blinded to any other possible relationships for themselves. They miss great opportunities to build new relationships. Regrettably, they remain stuck in the past. They refuse to shake the dust from their feet and go forward.

Because of the revelation from the Lord, I realized that I needed to move forward with my ministry. I could not live in the past. After I wept over the revelation about rejection and sorrow, I arrived home from the grocery store, and quickly went to my office to study the Word. I was open to hear from God.

EXAMPLES OF REJECTION

God began to show me from this Word how to move on from rejection. The Scripture that impressed me the most was 2 Timothy 4. In it, Paul describes the many people who abandoned him in his time of need. He mentions that *"Demas, because he loved this world, has deserted me."* He goes on to write, *"Crescens has gone to Galatia, and Titus to Dalmatia"* (verse 10). Then he mentions, *"Alexander the metalworker did me a great deal of harm"* (verse 14). Finally he exclaims, *"At my first defense, no one came to my support, but everyone deserted me. May it not be held against them"* (verse 16).

As you can see, Paul knew rejection. So how did he handle it? He writes: *"But the Lord stood at my side and gave me strength, so that through me the message might be fully proclaimed and all the Gentiles might hear it. And I was delivered from the lion's mouth"* (verse 17).

Paul knew that one had to be fully rejected before one could be fully accepted. He had to be fully rejected before he could fully proclaim the gospel so that *"all the Gentiles might hear it."*

He said, *"At my first defense, no one came to my support."* Paul had to first experience rejection before he could experience acceptance. His message was first rejected before it was accepted.

Moses tried to be Israel's leader before his time. He took matters into his own hands, and he failed miserably. Only when Israel fully rejected him would he become ready to be accepted as their leader. Moses went away to a hot desert for forty years. In that time, Israel forgot all about him. He had no public relations man to keep his name alive in the hearts of the Israelites. Sometimes, you will never be appreciated until people forget you. At the right time, God sent Moses back, and this time, the people accepted him. He had power to prove that God's hand was upon him.

Joseph is another great example of this principle in action. He had to be fully rejected by all before people would accept him. He was sold as a slave, falsely accused of rape, and abandoned in prison before he was exalted as the pharaoh's right-hand man.

Job also had to first be abandoned by his friends before he could be used to pray for them.

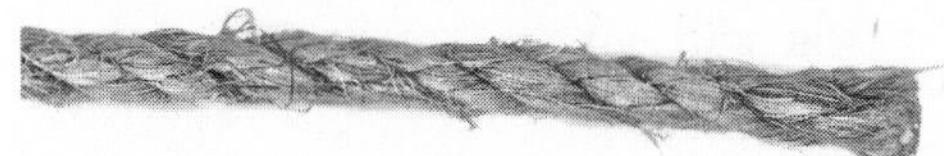

REJECTION WILL ONLY DESTROY YOU IF YOU REJECT YOURSELF. YOUR OPINION IS THE ONLY ONE THAT COUNTS. IF YOU REJECT YOURSELF, NO ONE'S OPINION WILL HELP. NEVER REJECT YOURSELF.

Jesus could not become Savior of the world until the world first rejected Him. Only when He was fully rejected could He be fully accepted. In truth, He went through a form of rejection that no one else has ever gone through. Not only did men reject him, even God rejected Him. He cried out on the cross, *"My God, my God, why have you forsaken me?"* (Matthew 27:46).

He experienced rejection—fully—so you and I could experience full acceptance by God. No matter what people have done to you, God still accepts you. He is with you.

Paul said, *"But the Lord stood at my side and gave me strength"* (2 Timothy 4:17). God will never abandon you. He will be there to give you strength.

Let me make this statement to you: Rejection will only destroy you if you reject yourself. Your opinion is the only one that counts. If you reject yourself, no one's opinion will help. Never reject yourself.

Unfortunately, that was what I was doing. I had begun to reject myself; I was defeating *myself*. No one can defeat you but *you*! So long as you believe that God is with you and that He is strengthening and loving you, you cannot lose. Accept yourself, so that when rejection comes, it will not destroy you.

FIFTEEN

LEARN FROM REJECTION

Read carefully again the list of the people who had abandoned Paul. It included not only bad people, but also good people. Titus left Paul for Dalmatia. Another friend, Crescens, went to Galatia.

These two good friends, Titus and Crescens, for reasons of their own, felt that they should leave Paul and go somewhere else.

As I read these passages, it dawned on me that not everyone who left my church was personally rejecting me. People had their reasons for leaving my church, and most had no malicious intent against me. Some wanted a bigger church with more ministries. Others wanted a smaller, cozier church. Still others preferred a different style of worship music. Perhaps some wanted a ministry with a different emphasis. Whatever the case, it did not matter. What mattered most was that I didn't think badly of them for leaving. I still had to consider them friends.

Sometimes, we take it too personally when people do not want to be with us. Not everyone who abandons or leaves you is necessarily a bad soul tie. Sometimes they were good for you. Don't judge everyone badly simply because they do not want to be with you anymore. They are still good people.

You might be a salesperson who has had many people reject your product. Just because they don't want to buy from you doesn't mean that they have rejected you. Learn to differentiate between people who are personally out to get you and those who simply don't want what you are providing. As you keep the doors open to them, they may very well return. This has happened to me many times over—people left the church only to return later.

Imagine, all this time I had felt like leaving the ministry because a few families left my church. You need to distinguish between those who hurt you through ignorance, and those who hurt you through malice. Sometimes people don't know they are hurting you. Jesus said on the cross, *"Father, forgive them, for they do not know what they are doing"* (Luke 23:34). They should not have crucified Christ; they were wrong, but they were ignorant as well.

As I look back over those dark years, I realize that many families left our church out of ignorance. They didn't really know what they were doing. They thought they were doing right, but they were deceived. Sometimes they were upset at me really for no good reason.

One family left because we started a bond program to finance our church. Another left because my family and I moved into a big home. Still others left because they weren't included in the decision-making process of our church. These are absurd reasons for leaving, but I realize that people do such things out of ignorance, not out of malice.

Learn to discern the difference between malice and ignorance. Be patient with those who are unaware of how they have hurt you.

DON'T BE SO SENSITIVE

People do not always reject you because of ignorance or malice; sometimes you deserve rejection. Ouch!

> *In the course of time Cain brought some of the fruits of the soil as an offering to the Lord. But Abel brought fat portions from some of the firstborn of his flock. The Lord looked with favor on Abel and his offering, but on Cain and his offering he did not look with favor. So Cain was very angry, and his face was downcast. Then the Lord said to Cain, "Why are you angry? Why is your face downcast? If you do what is right, will you not be accepted? But if you do not do what is right, sin is crouching at your door; it desires to have you, but you must master it."* (Genesis 4:3–7)

Cain's offering was rejected. As a result he became depressed and angry. As we have seen, these are classic symptoms of a rejected person.

God asks him, *"If you do what is right, will you not be accepted?"*

You might be able to sympathize with Cain. You think you are doing well, but you are not really giving God your best. So God and people don't accept what you have offered them. Don't get mad. Find out if you are giving your best.

Louisa May Alcott, author of *Little Women,* before writing that famous semi-autobiographical work, wrote another novel. She asked her fiancé his opinion of the book, and he told her that he did not like it. He said, "This book is not you." Louisa was furious. Later, she reconsidered his words, and realized that he was right. That's when she wrote her masterpiece. She learned from rejection.

Don't be too sensitive with criticism. Let it instruct you. Don't always interpret it as blatant rejection. Don't view constructive criticism as an attack against you, thereby letting it become a wound that creates the need for ungodly soul ties. People often get into bad relationships because they interpret criticism as a personal attack. They are looking for comfort in someone's arms. They are so hurt, they develop bad relationships in order to heal their wounds. That is the wrong way to handle corrective criticism.

PEOPLE OFTEN GET INTO BAD RELATIONSHIPS BECAUSE THEY INTERPRET CRITICISM AS A PERSONAL ATTACK. THEY ARE LOOKING FOR COMFORT IN SOMEONE'S ARMS. THEY ARE SO HURT, THEY DEVELOP BAD RELATIONSHIPS IN ORDER TO HEAL THEIR WOUNDS.

At times, I have to correct people in their job performance. I don't enjoy doing it, but I have to do it in order to help people reach their full potential. Once in a while, people are offended by my constructive criticism. Sometimes they leave. You will never get better if you are not willing to receive correction.

The reason you get hurt when people criticize you is because there is too much flesh in you. You have been crucified with Christ. You have died to the old man. Dead men don't hurt; kick a corpse and it won't cry. You must count yourself dead to the world. For example, if your parents favored your older sister, find out why. Maybe it was because she worked harder, got better grades, and made your parents proud.

Pastors need to learn why their church is not growing and why nobody accepts the gospel from them. It might be because rather than feeding the sheep, they beat them instead. If you're a salesperson, discover why you have not sold more. Maybe you are coming across wrong. Learn from your mistakes.

Don't kill the messenger. Don't let envy grip you like it did with Cain. Master the sin that has tried to rule you. You are not so perfect that you cannot grow to be better.

THE BRIGHT SIDE OF REJECTION

There is a bright side to rejection. I know that's hard to imagine. I mean, let's say you just asked a girl out and she turned you down. Actually, this happened to me before I got married. At the time, I was certainly not ready to see the good in it.

I worked at a pizza restaurant during my teen years. There was a very pretty girl who worked there whom I liked, but I never paid much attention to since I thought she was out of my league. This girl was not a born-again Christian, although I had once witnessed to her and prayed for her, and the Lord had healed her.

One day, a few of us employees were hanging around after the restaurant had closed. This girl—and I will never forget this—came to me with a different look. She stared into my eyes, with a sort of glazed look. She had had a bit too much to drink. Well…to be honest, she was flat-out drunk. She got real close and gave me one of those flirtatious, dreamy looks, then put her hands around my waist, pressed in close, and said, "Tom, with you being such a religious guy and me being such a sinner, I know we can be a real good match."

My mind was whirling, my heart was beating, and my spirit-man was saying, *Tell that Jezebel to get her hands off of you.* But my flesh was countering, *I like it!* I wish I could tell you that my spirit won. It did not.

I answered in an excited, high-pitch voice, "You really think so?" *Oh stupid me!*

The next day, I called to ask her out. She was too busy. I called the next day—still too busy. I was ready to call a third time, but then reality hit me: *She doesn't like me. She just said those things to me because she was drunk.*

Oh, at first I was hurt, but later I began to laugh. Can you imagine me dating a girl like that? My ministry would have been derailed.

As you can see, rejection worked out best. God had something better in store for me. I married a beautiful, godly Hispanic woman who has been a great help to my ministry.

In the same way, God had something better in mind for my church, too. I look back over those dark times in the ministry and I am thankful to God for some of the things that happened. I'm thankful that some people in my church left because it was for the best.

Remember Joseph in the Bible, the guy who was thrown into prison? He was probably wondering why God allowed him to remain in chains. *How is this going to work out for the good?*

Eventually, he met a fellow inmate who knew Pharaoh, and through him, Joseph was exalted to Pharaoh's right hand.

Later, when Joseph confronted his brothers, he cried, *"You intended to harm me, but God intended it for good to accomplish what is now being done"* (Genesis 50:20). Things worked out for the best.

Paul said this about his own problems:

> *Now I want you to know, brothers, that what has happened to me has really served to advance the gospel.... Because of my chains, most of the brothers in the Lord have been encouraged to speak the word of the God more courageously and fearlessly.* (Philippians 1:12, 14)

Paul saw his own prison experience as a means of furthering the gospel. He could have felt sorry for himself, but instead he chose to see the bright side of rejection.

Good even came out of the Jews rejecting Christ. *"He came to that which was his own, but his own did not receive him"* (John 1:11). What good came out of that? Paul said, *"Because of their transgression* [rejection of Christ], *salvation has come to the Gentiles"* (Romans 11:11). Their rejection is our opportunity. Good came out of Jesus' own people rejecting Him. Everything turned out for the good.

I know it's difficult to see the hand of God working in your life when you've been rejected and hurt so much, but rest assured, things will turn out for the good.

PART VI
DEVELOP SELF-ESTEEM IN CHRIST

SIXTEEN

SEE YOURSELF THROUGH GOD'S EYES

This book would not be complete if I did not share with you how to develop a proper self-image. The reason you may be tempted to develop relationships that are beneath you is because you do not feel worthy of top-notch people in your life. When you were abused and wounded by people, the first thing you lost was your self-esteem. And once you lose your self-esteem, you will allow anyone to mistreat you. You will become attracted to the wrong people.

This is what David felt: *"But I am a worm and not a man, scorned by men and despised by the people"* (Psalm 22:6). When you have been through so much pain, you don't even see yourself as human. You are less than human. David said, *"I am a worm."* Why? Because people despised him. You lose a proper image of yourself because of the pain you have experienced.

Rosie Rivera, the sister of the famed Latin singer, Jenni Rivera, knows firsthand how one's self-image can be destroyed by another. Her father always called her "princess," but after what she went through she felt more like a "witch." When she was only eight years old, she was sexually molested by Jenni's husband, Trino. The abuse continued for three years. One day, she told her sister and parents about what was happening to her. Thankfully, they ultimately believed her. Trino, however, escaped from the authorities and was a fugitive for eighteen years. Eventually, he was caught, tried, and convicted.

For Rosie, however, the wounds he caused remained far beyond his conviction. Her relationship with Christ was damaged. She was filled with bitterness and vengeance. She became promiscuous and drank heavily. One day, she found herself alone on the streets after spending the entire night at a nightclub. Her clothes were torn, her hair was disheveled, and she sat on the curb, contemplating her life. Thoughts of suicide began to overtake her. Yet, like the prodigal son in the Bible, she decided to return home. That morning, she went to church with her parents. There she confessed her sins to God and was released from her bitterness. It was there she felt the love of God again. She could almost hear Him whisper, *"You are my princess!"*

It wasn't easy, but she turned her life over to God. Since then, she has become a bold witness for Christ. She doesn't care what others think about her. She has learned to see herself through her Father's eyes. She is a princess before God.

JESSICA'S STORY

Jessica was a young Puerto Rican child living in South Florida. At the age of five, she was approached by a man who offered her a gift. She was excited to receive it. He told her to close her eyes, and she did. He told her to hold out her hand. When she did, she felt something, but not what she expected. She opened her eyes and screamed because the man had pulled out his genitals and put them in her hands!

As you can imagine, this was traumatic event for Jessica. This terrible incident caused her to grow up with negative and fearful feelings. She became disgusted with men, specifically with male genitalia. As a result, she began to question her sexual identity.

At this point, Jessica was invited to a Spirit-filled church, where she saw people lifting their hands to praise God. She had never witnessed this before, but she loved it. Something in her soul was gripped. Without understanding the meaning of praise and worship, she joined in the crowd and began to praise God. She lifted her hands as tears began to stream down her face. It was there she felt the unconditional, true love of a Man—Jesus, the God-man. By the end of the service, she had surrendered her life to Jesus. She began to weep as she prayed and gave her life to Him. She saw that the inner pain she had experienced over that sexual molestation had left her. She no longer felt pain and disgust. She only felt God's love. Jessica was healed.

Hopefully, by this time in this book, you have experienced inner healing. Your broken heart has been mended like Rosie's and Jessica's. Listen, Satan will not give up. He knows what has worked in the past, and he will try it again. You can't be vulnerable to his attacks. The best way to guard against negative soul ties is to develop a proper self-image.

It is easy to develop a negative self-image, primarily because of the negative soul ties you have formed in the past. People put you down—parents, siblings, peers, teachers, bosses, and spouses. But you cannot let their image of you become the image that you have of yourself.

SATAN WILL NOT GIVE UP. HE KNOWS WHAT HAS WORKED IN THE PAST, AND HE WILL TRY IT AGAIN. YOU CAN'T BE VULNERABLE TO HIS ATTACKS. THE BEST WAY TO GUARD AGAINST NEGATIVE SOUL TIES IS TO DEVELOP A PROPER SELF-IMAGE.

The Bible teaches that God sees you differently than others do. God looks at you, not through your natural self, but through your spiritual self. The gospel reveals what God did for you and who He says you are in Christ. Through the sacrifice of Christ, and through the words God has spoken over your life, you can create a right "*in Christ*" image of yourself. Let me explain the importance of the right "*in Christ*" self-image and how it will empower you to overcome any problem in your life.

GRASSHOPPER IMAGE

Twelve spies arrived back in the camp. They had hoped to find some weakness in their enemies that would allow them to conquer the land, but they had no such luck. The enemies were strong and powerful. Ten spies shrunk away from God's promises. God had said that their nation would possess this land, but they believed more in what they saw than in what God had spoken. One of the spies, however, named Caleb, refused to doubt God's promises.

> *Then Caleb silenced the people before Moses and said, "We should go up and take possession of the land, for we can certainly do it." But the men who had gone up with him said, "We can't attack those people; they are stronger than we are." And they spread among the Israelites a bad report about the land they had explored. They said, "The land we explored devours those living in it. All the people we saw there are of great size. We saw the Nephilim there (the descendants of Anak come from the Nephilim). We seemed like grasshoppers in our own eyes, and we looked the same to them."* (Numbers 13:30–33)

Notice the problem of the ten spies. They *"seemed like grasshoppers in* [their] *own eyes."* They had no confidence in their ability to defeat the enemy. There is nothing wrong with having a self-confidence that is rooted in God's Word. Pride is when you think you can accomplish great things on your *own*, without God.

AS YOU DEVELOP A RIGHT IMAGE OF YOURSELF, YOU WILL NOT LET OTHERS DEFEAT YOU.

Caleb, on the other hand, was righteously self-confident! He boldly declared, *"We can certainly do it!"* Of course he knew it would only be possible with God's help, but what is the point of saying that God can do anything if you won't let Him use you? Caleb knew that God would not defeat their enemies if they did not courageously put forth the effort. This is where self-esteem comes in. You must believe that God can use you to obtain victory in life.

As you develop a right image of yourself, you will not let others defeat you. Caleb was never going to experience subjugation at the hands of the Nephilim or anyone else in the land. Why? Because he did not see himself as a grasshopper. Maybe his enemies were trying to destroy his strong image of himself, but Caleb would not let them. He believed in the God who believed in him! You must say that *"I can do all things through Christ who strengthens me"* (Philippians 4:13 NKJV). You must break out of your grasshopper image.

Psychologists call the grasshopper image *inferiority*. The word is a psychological term and thus is not in the Bible. Some people think that if it is not in the Bible, it is not true. Well, the word *cancer* is not found in Scripture, yet the Bible speaks of it in other ways. Similarly, instead of using the modern psychological term "inferiority," the Bible uses other terms that mean the same thing. Here are some of those terms.

FALSE HUMILITY

Colossians 2:18 says, *"Do not let anyone who delights in false humility and the worship of angels disqualify you for the prize."* The reason the Bible mentions humility in terms of "true" or "false" is because many are confused as to the real meaning of humility. Some think they are humble if they think badly of themselves, when in reality, that is false humility. You are not humble if you let the hard things of the past dictate your current image of yourself. If there is such a thing as false humility, there must also be true humility. Titus 3:2 says to *"show true humility toward all men."*

FEAR OF MAN

Proverbs 29:25 says, *"Fear of man will prove to be a snare."* You only fear those whom you believe to be greater than you. This is what the ten spies clearly did; they feared their enemies more than they trusted God.

Stop fearing the abuse of others. Stop letting them dictate to you your view of yourself. You deserve better than someone who beats you up; you deserve better than someone who does not believe in you. God believes in you. Learn to see yourself as God sees you.

GUILT

Clearly the gospel deals with guilt. Guilt is another aspect of inferiority.

You are forgiven! Don't live in guilt anymore. Yes, you made your share of mistakes—who hasn't? But accept God's forgiveness.

First John 3:19–20 says, *"This then is how we know that we belong to the truth, and how we set our hearts at rest in his presence whenever our hearts condemn us. For God is greater than our hearts, and he knows everything."* John urged us not to believe everything our *"hearts"* tell us. The word *"hearts"* refers to your emotions. Even when you feel condemned, John reminds you that God is greater than your critical spirit. God may forgive you, yet you may still be holding sins against yourself. You should learn to accept God's forgiveness instead of beating yourself up for your past.

SHAME

Surely shame is universal. When one is shamed, he or she blushes. Blushing is a sign of inferiority. Who does not feel bad about himself when he or she is shamed? It is easy to allow the sexual molestation, the rape, and the divorce to shame you. Don't let it!

In the next chapter, we'll explore exactly how we can develop a proper self-image of ourselves.

SEVENTEEN

MIRROR, MIRROR ON THE WALL

Anyone who listens to the word but does not do what it says is like a man who looks at his face in a mirror and, after looking at himself, goes away and immediately forgets what he looks like. But the man who looks intently into the perfect law that gives freedom, and continues to do this, not forgetting what he has heard, but doing it—he will be blessed in what he does. (James 1:23–25)

What is the purpose of a mirror? It is to show you what you look like. Do you remember the story of Snow White? Her wicked stepmother said to the mirror, "Mirror, mirror on the wall, who's the fairest of them all?" The mirror would then give her the answer. Even in fairy-tale reality, a mirror talks back to us. The mirror tells you who you are! James likens God's Word to a mirror, because in the same way, God tells you who you are!

You have voices echoing through your mind, like a song on repeat, constantly telling you who you are. Those voices could be from negative soul ties in the past. They could be from authority figures—parents, teachers, ministers, peers—and they often speak lies. (Again, this is not the same as constructive criticism, which you also need to become a better person.) Your goal is to differentiate between the lies you have accepted and the truth of the gospel. Don't hold to the lies of the enemy. Don't allow the devil to destroy your sense of self-esteem and self-worth.

Notice that James says when you *"do"* what the Word says, you will be *"blessed in what"* you do. It is not simply hearing the Word that changes your image, but specifically doing it. You feel good about yourself when you have acted on the Word of God.

If you continue living in a relationship that is not God-honoring, you will not feel good about yourself. You will also not feel good about yourself when you do not live a life of love and forgive others, even those who have hurt you.

I always feel good about myself when I forgive, love others, and do them good. Yet, I feel rotten when I am embittered or mean to others. There is no point in trying to develop a positive self-image without practicing the Word.

The Word—like a mirror—will point out changes you need to make. You look into a mirror and notice that your hair is messed up. The mirror will help you comb it and make yourself look better, and, thus, feel better about yourself. In the same way, the Bible often points out the changes you need to make, not so that God can condemn you, but so that you can change. When you change, it makes you feel good about yourself.

I LOOK GOOD IN CHRIST

When I was young, every year I would go to our city's amusement park. The one thing I remember is the funny mirror. On one side of the mirror, I looked short and fat, while on the other side, I appeared tall and skinny. Because of my short stature, I preferred to look at myself in the tall side!

A mirror does not necessarily reflect exactly what you look like, but what the maker of the mirror wants you to see. The mirror of God's Word not only reflects what you should look like to yourself and others, but it shows you how God sees you in Christ.

Former NFL quarterback Tim Tebow went through an identity crisis when he was cut from the New England Patriots. His life, up to that point, had been completely centered on football and specifically on being a quarterback. Suddenly, still in his early twenties, he was out of football. He was deemed not good enough to be a quarterback in the NFL. How did he get through it? He writes,

> I like to say that identity comes not necessarily from who we are, but from whose we are.
>
> I am a child of God. My foundation for who I am is grounded in my faith. In a God who loves me. In a God who gives me purpose. In a God who sees the big picture. In a God who always has a greater plan.
>
> Who am I? I am the object of his love.
>
> That's a big deal.[7]

It is a big deal. You need to see yourself from God's standpoint. He does not look at you from a natural standpoint—such

---

7. Tim Tebow, *Shaken: Discovering Your True Identity in the Midst of Life's Storms* (New York: WaterBrook, 2016), 28.

as how well you behave—but through redemption. He sees that you are complete in Christ. Too many times, instead of looking at yourself from the standpoint of what the Bible says about you, you look at yourself through the eyes of your own natural understanding. When you do that, you can't see the reality of what God has done for you because you are not seeing yourself in Christ.

Just as some people look good "in red," you look a whole lot better "in Christ." The phrase "in Christ" unlocks the mystery of the Bible, and is the key that opens up to you all the treasures of heaven. I challenge you to do something I learned to do years ago: read through the New Testament and highlight or underline phrases such as "in Christ," "in Him," "in the beloved," "in whom," "through Christ," "because of Christ," "with Christ," or simply any expression that reveals who you are, what you can do, and what you have as a believer.

After marking those verses, turn them into a positive self-proclamation. For example: *"Therefore, if anyone is in Christ, he is a new creation; the old has gone, the new has come!"* (2 Corinthians 5:17). Take this Scripture and say out loud about yourself: "I am a new creation; the old has gone, and the new has come!"

Do this every day. Find other verses like this and make them into positive proclamations. Saying these Scriptures over your life for the rest of your life will change your self-image into an "in Christ" positive image. No matter what words people have spoken over your life, no matter how they have hurt you, the Word of God can break any grasshopper image and bring you victory in Christ. It will keep you from a broken heart.

Just make sure you are looking into the right mirror.

EIGHTEEN

WHO DO YOU THINK YOU ARE?

My friend Pastor Francis grew up with a negative self-image. It started when he was young and a ten-year-old girl told him, "You are ugly!"

Those words stuck in his soul. He felt ugly; he believed he was ugly. He never thought another girl would ever want to date him. So he never asked any girl out during his whole time in high school.

Then, one day, during his senior year, a friend told him that the prettiest girl in school wanted Francis to take her to the senior prom. His friend said that she had turned down other dates with the hope that he would ask her. Francis couldn't believe it!

Eventually, Francis nervously went to the girl and shyly said, "I heard that you wanted to go to the prom with me. Is that really true?"

She said, "Of course. I would love to go with the most handsome guy in school."

"What, *me*? The most handsome?"

"Yes. Every girl here knows that!"

For the first time, Francis saw himself as handsome. He realized that the ten-year-old girl had lied to him. He wasn't ugly after all.

Who has been lying to you? Who have you allowed to be your mirror? Who have you allowed to tell you who you are? What is the information you have used to establish your identity?

IDENTITY CRISIS

No doubt you have heard these judgmental words: "Who do you think you are?"

There are a myriad of answers you can reply when asked this question. You can focus on your natural self, and say, "I am a son, or daughter, or teacher, or entrepreneur, an artist, a mom, a dad, etc." Often, the world looks to label people by what they do. In our society, what you do and how you feel equals who you are. The world will tell you self-esteem is how much you *feel* valued, loved, and accepted by others. The way others see you, and the way you see yourself, is where you find your worth, they say. This is what Pastor Francis did when he allowed another person's view to taint his view of himself.

Many people's identities stem from their earthly characteristics: gender, race, ethnicity, sexual orientation, wealth, or family. People think these characteristics are what define them.

If any of these characteristics are challenged or are taken away, people feel as if they are going through a crisis—an identity crisis. But this approach to self-esteem is merely the world's way of self-esteem—and God is left out of the equation.

YOU ARE A MIRROR TO REFLECT GOD'S GLORY; YOU ARE NOT YOUR *OWN* MIRROR. THE WORLD'S MIRROR CANNOT PRESENT A TRUE "IN CHRIST" IMAGE OF YOURSELF. IT WILL CONCENTRATE TOO MUCH ON YOUR NATURAL LOOKS, MONEY, AND ABILITIES.

A BIBLICAL VIEW

So what does the Bible say about self-esteem, and about who you are?

To find a true, biblical identity, you should start at the beginning.

> *Then God said, "Let us make man in our image, in our likeness, and let them rule over the fish of the sea and the birds of the air, over the livestock, over all the earth, and over all the creatures that move along the ground." So God created man in his own image, in the image of God he created him; male and female he created them.*
>
> (Genesis 1:26–27)

First of all, if you want to know who you truly are, you must look at your relationship with God. You don't know who you are by looking at your relationship with others. As important as human relationships are, that is not where you should get your identity. You are a mirror to reflect God's glory; you are not your *own* mirror. The world's mirror cannot present a true "in Christ" image of yourself. It will concentrate too much on your natural looks, money, and abilities.

The devil likes to divert you from reflecting God's image. He's been using the same trap since the beginning, and he continues to use it today. How did he tempt Adam and Eve, the first humans created by God to reflect His image? Genesis 3:5 shows Satan enticing Adam and Eve: *"For God knows that when you eat of it* (the fruit from the tree of the knowledge of good and evil) *your eyes will be opened, and you will be like God, knowing good and evil."*

Satan created the first identity crisis. The reason why knowing who you are is so important is because *what you do* flows from *who you are.* Adam and Eve ate the fruit because they forgot *who they were.* They forgot that mankind was already *"like God."* They wanted to be more than a reflection. They wanted to form their own identity apart from God, and this was sinful. This is what bad soul ties do. Negative soul ties try to become your mirror. They say, "Who do you think you are? You will amount to nothing without me. No one will love you!"

Then, when someone abuses you, and you allow it to continue, the abuser will try to get you to see yourself—define yourself—based on his or her relationship with you. And this is deadly.

BORN INTO THE HUMAN FAMILY

You are born naturally into Adam's family. You share his sinful, selfish, and identity-crisis nature. You were dead in sin because of Adam, but 1 Corinthians 15:22 gives you hope: *"For as in Adam all die, so in Christ all will be made alive."*

When a team captain calls heads or tails before the coin toss of a football game, his call affects the whole team. So Adam's choice affected all of humanity. But thankfully, because Jesus chose to die on the cross for our sins, His choice also affects whoever believes in Him. In Adam, there is condemnation; but in Christ, there is salvation.

BORN AGAIN IN CHRIST

Paul understood the meaning of an identity crisis when he spoke to the church at Ephesus. The people in this church were looking outside of God for their worth, self-esteem, and identity. In his letter to the Ephesians, Paul wrote of believers as being *"in Christ," "in Him," "in the beloved,"* or some other variation of these words a total of twenty-two times. In sum, Paul used the phrase *"in Christ,"* or its variations, in all of his letters two hundred sixteen times. He knew we were going to forget our identity. He knew we needed to remember our true identity.

Who are you?

WHEN GOD SEES YOU, HE SEES CHRIST. HE ATTRIBUTES TO YOU EVERYTHING THAT CHRIST HAS AND IS—RIGHTEOUSNESS, HOLINESS, AND WISDOM. DO NOT VIEW YOURSELF APART FROM CHRIST.

YOU ARE IN CHRIST

To be in Christ is to be sheltered in Him. You are not left alone without shelter. To be in Christ doesn't mean that you are one person and Christ is another person. It means that your identity becomes wrapped up in Christ's identity. *"As* [Christ] *is, so are we in this world"* (1 John 4:17 KJV). You cannot see yourself as different from Christ. Christ is God's Son; you are God's child. Christ is loved; you are loved. Christ is holy; you are holy.

When God sees you, He sees Christ. He attributes to you everything that Christ has and is—righteousness, holiness, and wisdom. Do not view yourself apart from Christ. Expect God to treat you in the same way He treated Jesus Christ. He sees you like He sees Him.

Listen to what Paul says about this.

1. IN CHRIST, YOU ARE A SAINT

> *Paul, an apostle of Christ Jesus by the will of God, to the saints in Ephesus, the faithful in Christ Jesus: Grace and peace to you from God our Father and the Lord Jesus Christ.* (Ephesians 1:1–2)

The first identity Paul mentions to those *"in Christ"* is that of being saints. He says, *"to the saints in Ephesus."* But surely there were all types of believers in Ephesus! Some were mature in their faith, some were weak. Paul, however, does not make any sort of distinction between the mature and the new believers. He calls them all saints.

When I was young, I accepted the designation of saint. I used to work at a restaurant and after helping an employee, he told me, "I will ask God to make you a saint!"

I replied, "You don't have to. I already am."

Of course, he was shocked! A saint? How could I be saint? Didn't it take some miraculous sign or wonder for me to be considered a saint? What he didn't know was that in Christ, we are all saints.

Now, I know what you're thinking. "How can I be a saint? I sin all the time! Don't you know how bad I am? Saints don't act like me."

Friend, how can you expect to act like a saint if you don't even believe you are one? If you believe you are a sinner, you're going to walk like a sinner under condemnation. Focusing on your sin will leave you in despair. Don't do that! If you are saved, then you are saint. God has wiped away your iniquities.

THE BAD NEWS IS THAT YOU STILL SIN. BUT YOU'VE FORGOTTEN THE GOOD NEWS–YOU'RE IN CHRIST NOW! AND IN CHRIST, YOUR SIN DOES NOT DEFINE YOU; IT IS NO LONGER A PART OF YOUR IDENTITY.

Yes, the bad news is that you still sin. But you've forgotten the good news—you're in Christ now! And in Christ, your sin does not define you; it is no longer a part of your identity. It does not matter how you feel or what others say; God says you are a saint.

This is not the only thing you are though. Let's continue reading Paul's words to the Ephesians.

Who are you?

2. IN CHRIST, YOU ARE BLESSED

Praise be to the God and Father of our Lord Jesus Christ, who has blessed us in the heavenly realms with every spiritual blessing in Christ. (Ephesians 1:3)

It says that God blessed us with spiritual blessings. In interpreting this, some might think we should not expect physical blessings, like health, money, or inner healing.

But when God gives us something, even something physical, it automatically qualifies as a spiritual blessing, as it says in James 1:17: *"Every good and perfect gift is from above, coming down from the Father of the heavenly lights, who does not change like shifting shadows."*

Your life? A gift from God.

Your job? A gift from God.

Your family? A gift from God.

What are some of the blessings God has given you?

ADOPTION

He predestined us to be adopted as his sons through Jesus Christ, in accordance with his pleasure and will.

(Ephesians 1:5)

An orphan looks forward to being adopted. But first they must be chosen. You are chosen by God! He picked you. Maybe others have rejected you, but God has accepted you. He adopted you into His family. It wasn't an accident.

ACCEPTANCE

Wherein he hath made us accepted in the beloved.

(Ephesians 1:6 KJV)

Maybe your father and mother did not accept you. Maybe your spouse or former spouse did not accept you. What does it matter? When God accepts you, you are accepted. He does not reject you.

God accepts you because you accepted His Son. You are *"accepted in the beloved."* Since you love God's Son, God accepts you as His own. This Scripture should drive out all rejection from your life.

GRACE

In accordance with the riches of God's grace that he lavished on us.... (Ephesians 1:7–8)

Why would a holy God adopt a sinner like you? Grace. This is free, not earned. Before you could do anything to show the Lord you loved and obeyed Him, He blesses you by showing you grace.

REDEMPTION

In him we have redemption through his blood.... (Ephesians 1:7)

Israel knows what it's like to be redeemed or set free. They were in slavery in Egypt until God redeemed them. He delivered them from their bondage. Just as they were redeemed, God has also broken the bondage of sin from your life. Because of this, even the effects of sin are broken. You have the legal right to break any ungodly soul ties that have tried to put you in bondage.

FORGIVENESS

Have you ever been of ashamed of the words you've spoken or the deeds you've done? Maybe there is someone you've hurt, or people you've grieved. One blessing you have in Christ is that of forgiveness. He has taken your shame and has called you pure.

WISDOM AND UNDERSTANDING

> *...that he lavished on us with all wisdom and understanding.* (Ephesians 1:8)

Have people called you stupid? They lied. Einstein was considered stupid by many people when he was young. Their viewpoint was wrong!

Jesus has lavished wisdom on you. You are not dumb. Wisdom guides you to make the right, God-honoring choices. "*Understanding*" helps you to know why you should do so. These two blessings will affect your relationships. You will have wisdom to make the right, God-honoring soul ties, instead of the toxic ones of your past.

THE HOLY SPIRIT

> *Having believed, you were marked in him with a seal, the promised Holy Spirit, who is a deposit guaranteeing our inheritance until the redemption of those who are God's possession—to the praise of his glory.* (Ephesians 1:13–14)

The Holy Spirit is the executor of the blessings. He causes the blessings to arrive in your life. He gives the gift of tongues, prophesy, and miracles. He gives you health and restoration.

In Christ, you are blessed! But this is not all!

Who are you?

3. IN CHRIST, YOU ARE CALLED

> *I keep asking that the God of our Lord Jesus Christ, the glorious Father, may give you the Spirit of wisdom and*

revelation, so that you may know him better. I pray also that the eyes of your heart may be enlightened in order that you may know the hope to which he has called you, the riches of his glorious inheritance in the saints, and his incomparably great power for us who believe. (Ephesians 1:17–19)

At one point in your life, you may have asked yourself, "What is my calling, my purpose?"

Bishop T. D. Jakes says that the number one question he gets from people is, "How can I know my purpose?" Your purpose is God's call on your life.

A calling is your vocation; it brings purpose to your life, and helps you to know that you are not wasting your life on earth. You are talented and gifted; maybe you don't have a silver tongue, but you have other gifts. Don't let others tell you that you don't have anything to offer.

The thing about being called by God is that you are constantly being called. Your calling is fluid. There is a destination God has in mind for you, and you should always be headed toward it. You are *always* being called, but toxic soul ties will lead you away from your purpose.

My story is like a lot of people's. It didn't begin by waking up one morning as the pastor I knew I was meant to be. I've had many jobs in my lifetime, but I always knew that I was called to proclaim the gospel and to set people free. Though I am now bishop of a large church and diocese, my life wasn't always like this.

When I first became a Christian, I was an employee in a restaurant. While working outside of the church, I volunteered as a children's church aide. Soon, the church promoted me to become a children's church teacher. Then, I was the Sunday school superintendent. Being faithful wherever God called me at the time eventually led me to becoming pastor of a small church. I stayed faithful and soon hosted a Christian program on a radio station. I moved on to TV and then started writing books. What started as small beginnings has now led me to being a bishop. And yet, this is still not the end! Right now, I am faithful as a bishop, but who knows where God will lead me next?

All those times, I was faithful to the "small" things. God called me to those small responsibilities. The great thing is that every believer is called, not just those with tremendous business skills or great influence. Your calling continues as long as God has given you breath. You are always being called to something, even if it is not the "something" you had in mind. God has orchestrated the right people in your life to help bring you into your calling. Don't let negative people divert you from your calling.

Who are you?

4. IN CHRIST, YOU ARE ALIVE

So, in Christ, you know that you are a saint, blessed with all the heavenly blessings, and that you are continually called. Is there anything else?

> *As for you, you were dead in your transgressions and sins.... But because of his great love for us, God, who is rich in mercy, made us alive with Christ.* (Ephesians 2:1, 4–5)

On TV, there is a commercial I love that asks kids a series of rather simple questions. For example, the adult asks, "Which is better: faster or slower?" All of the kids quickly reply, "Faster!" as if there is no other option.

I have a question to ask you. Which is better: being alive or being dead?

To be made alive means that we were once *not* alive. We were dead.

The world itself is full of the walking dead. The world will say that you can do whatever you want because nothing matters. The world will tell you that getting drunk and doing drugs will make you happy. Those people who believe the world's lies are the walking dead. They are dead in their sins, thinking that whatever they do will make them feel alive.

If you are in Christ, you are already alive! You do not need things of this world to make you feel alive, because you are alive in Christ! You don't need that bad relationship; you can live without him or her. Living in sin will not make you feel more alive!

YOU DO NOT NEED THINGS OF THIS WORLD TO MAKE YOU FEEL ALIVE, BECAUSE YOU ARE ALIVE IN CHRIST! YOU DON'T NEED THAT BAD RELATIONSHIP; YOU CAN LIVE WITHOUT HIM OR HER. LIVING IN SIN WILL NOT MAKE YOU FEEL MORE ALIVE!

In the past, you were one of them: the walking dead. When I see zombies in a movie, I always cheer for the people who are alive to survive and stay alive! No one in the movies wants to be a zombie; they keep running to escape. The walking dead are not to be admired. Yet when you were dead before Christ, you used to follow these walking dead. Now that you are alive, do not follow their ways! The zombies are the bad, toxic soul ties that will kill your self-esteem in Christ. Survive and stay alive!

THE CHURCH LEADS THE WAY

In history, the church has always been at the forefront of change. The church has continually stood up for civil rights. Christians were at the forefront of the movement to end slavery. Christians have continually stood up for women's rights. Today, Christians are leading the way to end abortion, to stand up for traditional marriage, and to combat pornography and sex trafficking. Christians are leading the way because God has made them alive!

We are not the walking dead, living for temporary pleasures. There is more to this life than what we can see; there is a spiritual battle going on in our land. Who are you going to follow in this battle?

Let's return to the question even children know the answer to: Which is better? Being alive or being dead? Alive! And indeed, in Christ, you are made alive.

You may look like a father or a mother. You may look wealthy or poor. But in Christ, we are all the same. We are more than what meets the eye. The final question remains: Who are you?

You are a saint.

You are blessed.

You are called.

You are alive.

CONCLUSION

I hope that you have broken ungodly soul ties and experienced inner healing. Now it is time to build your self-esteem in Christ. As you do, you will never allow others to put you down. You will stand up for yourself and live a healthy and strong life in Christ.

It does not matter what people say about you; it matters only what you say about yourself. Say what God says. I want you to take the following positive affirmations based on the Word of God, and speak it out loud to yourself. Do it not just once, but as often as you need to change your image of yourself. You will especially need to do this when people speak terrible things about you. Say this:

I am a New Creation in Christ Jesus. I am not a worm. I am a child of the living God. God has accepted me in Christ. I refuse to have a grasshopper image of myself. I see myself as a giant in Christ. I am well able to inherit all God's promises for my life.

I will not fear people. I will not feel guilt over the forgiven sins of my past. I reject feelings of shame over my past, or any feelings of shame that people try to put on me. I look into God's mirror and I see Christ's image of me.

I will not be a forgetful hearer of God's Word, but I will be a doer of God's Word. I will not sink into sinful habits. My foundation is grounded in my faith in God.

I am the object of God's love. I am born again in Christ. I am a saint. I am blessed with spiritual blessings in heavenly places in Christ. I am adopted as a child of God into God's family. God picked me to be in His family. He wants me as His child. God has lavished on me the riches of His grace. I am redeemed by the blood of Jesus Christ.

I have been forgiven, and I forgive others. I am smart. I have wisdom and understanding through the Holy Spirit. I am sealed by God. I belong to Him, and to no one else. God has called me to an eternal hope. I have an inheritance now in this life. I have the power of God residing in me. This power is God's resurrection power. I am alive with Christ. I have been made to sit with Christ in heavenly places. The devil and all toxic soul ties are under my feet.

How does it feel to say this? I am sure you feel more confident in your life. God wants you to feel this confidence. As you change your self-esteem, you will find yourself less attracted to broken people. You will love them in Christ. You will have compassion for them and pray for them, but you will no longer be attracted to them. Instead, you will feel connected with other individuals who are healthy and whole.

As you become whole yourself, you will no longer desire friendships, romantic or otherwise, with people who want to try to tear you down. You are now free of all toxic soul ties. You have now embarked on becoming a whole person in Christ.

> *So if the Son sets you free, you will be free indeed.*
>
> (John 8:36)

Alleluia!

ABOUT THE AUTHOR

Tom Brown is best known for his deliverance ministry. Millions have seen him on ABC's *20/20*, as well as on MSNBC and the History Channel. He is a noted conference speaker, prolific author, and committed pastor. His award-winning Internet site, www.tbm.org, reaches more than a million people a year. His books published by Whitaker House are *You Can Predict Your Future; Devil, Demons, and Spiritual Warfare; Breaking Curses, Experiencing Healing; Prayers That Get Results;* and *Spiritual Gifts for Spiritual Warfare.* Tom resides in El Paso, Texas, with his beautiful wife, Sonia. They have three children together and are empty nesters.